THE SCHOOL OF LIFE is dedicated to exploring life's big questions: *How can we fulfill our potential? Can work be inspiring? Why does community matter? Can relationships last a lifetime?* We don't have all the answers, but we will direct you toward a variety of useful ideas—from philosophy to literature, psychology to the visual arts—that are guaranteed to stimulate, provoke, nourish, and console.

THESCHOOLOFLIFE.COM

"In an age of moral and practical confusions, the self-help book is crying out to be redesigned and rehabilitated. The School of Life announces a rebirth with a series that examines the great issues of life, including money, sanity, work, technology, and the desire to alter the world for the better."

—ALAIN DE BOTTON,
THE SCHOOL OF LIFE SERIES EDITOR

About the Author

EVA HOFFMAN is an internationally known writer and academic. She has worked as a senior editor at *The New York Times*, and has presented radio programmes on the BBC. Her books include *Lost in Translation*, *Shtetl* and *Time*, as well as two novels, *The Secret* and *Illuminations*.

Also by Eva Hoffman

Time

Illuminations

*After Such Knowledge: Memory, History and the
Legacy of the Holocaust*

The Secret

*Shtetl: The Life and Death of a Small Town and the
World of Polish Jews*

*Exit into History: A Journey Through the New
Eastern Europe*

Lost in Translation: A Life in a New Language

HOW TO BE BORED

HOW TO BE BORED

Eva Hoffman

PICADOR

New York

picadorusa.com • picadorbookroom.tumblr.com
twitter.com/picadorusa • facebook.com/picadorusa

Picador® is a U.S. registered trademark and is used by Macmillan Publishing Group, LLC, under license from Pan Books Limited.

For book club information, please visit facebook.com/picadorbookclub or e-mail marketing@picadorusa.com.

Designed by Steven Seighman

The photographic credits starting on page 169 constitute an extension of this copyright page.

Library of Congress Cataloging-in-Publication Data

Names: Hoffman, Eva, 1945– author.
Title: How to be bored / Eva Hoffman.
Description: First U.S. edition. | New York : Picador, [2017]
Identifiers: LCCN 2016039169 (print) | LCCN 2016044813 (e-book) | ISBN 9781250078674 (hardcover) | ISBN 9781250078681 (e-book)
Subjects: LCSH: Boredom.
Classification: LCC BF575.B67 H64 2017 (print) | LCC BF575.B67 (e-book) | DDC 152.4—dc23
LC record available at https://lccn.loc.gov/2016039169

Our books may be purchased in bulk for promotional, educational, or business use. Please contact your local bookseller or the Macmillan Corporate and Premium Sales Department at 1-800-221-7945, extension 5442, or by e-mail at MacmillanSpecialMarkets@macmillan.com.

Originally published in Great Britain by Macmillan, an imprint of Pan Macmillan

First U.S. Edition: January 2017

10 9 8 7 6 5 4 3 2 1

Contents

I.   The Problem   1
1.   Hyperactivity and Its Discontents   3
2.   Challenges of Choice   15

II. Leisure   25
3.   Idleness   27
4.   Introspection   37
5.   Imaginative Exploration   71
6.   Contemplative Concentration   99
7.   Choosing from Within   105

III. Engagement   121
8.   Work   127
9.   Relationships   137
10. Creative Play   149

Conclusion   157

x Contents

Homework   159

Photographic Credits and
Permissions Acknowledgements   169

I. The Problem

1. Hyperactivity and Its Discontents

You've had a normal, and normally harried, day at the office. Urgent decisions had to be made on the hoof, and an awkward exchange with your boss left you a bit rattled. You'll have to figure out later what it was about. On the way home, on the underground, you open your favourite computer game on your smartphone. Several text messages have arrived from your friends suggesting the evening's activities; you'll have to check out the various entertainment venues. At home, you text your partner to say where to meet you later, and try to answer as many emails as possible before going out. The evening is lively and full of laughs, and it goes on till quite late that night. Back home, you look at the Twitter messages which have accumulated during the evening. Some left-over dross of the day is nagging at you, and as you crash for the night, you feel an odd sense of uncertainty. Surely, your day was busy and exciting. Why, then, do you feel as if you somehow missed it, as if it didn't leave anything behind?

* * *

This is a book about a problem which is elusive partly because it is so pervasive. It is a problem of excessive busyness and overfilled schedules, and their effects on our mental and emotional lives. It is also about how we might address and counter such problems, for the sake of experiencing our lives more fully.

There have been periods when the great difficulty, at least for some people and social classes, was having too much time on their hands, and the ever-present danger of boredom. Here is Søren Kierkegaard, the nineteenth-century Danish philosopher, on the subject: 'How dreadful boredom is – how dreadfully boring . . . I lie prostrate, inert; the only thing I see is emptiness, the only thing I live on is emptiness, the only thing I move in is emptiness.'

Lethargic inactivity can be debilitating and depressing; but for us, the pendulum has swung far in the other direction. We live in a hectic, hyperactive, over-stimulated age. Since the introduction of the internet and digital technologies, we have infinite quanta of information, visual imagery, personal communications and impersonal text available to us anywhere and at any time. In the non-virtual realm, too, our world offers a constant supply of activity, diversion and stimulation. In shops throbbing with crowds and bright lights, we can buy anything we can – or can't – imagine. At every turn, we are presented with a mind-boggling quantity of entertainment, high and low: YouTube, music festivals, art exhibitions.

The busyness of our lives is partly a response to these conditions, and to the demands of our complex, highly competitive societies. Most of us need to work hard in order to ensure a livelihood and basic comforts for ourselves and our families; and if we are to succeed, we are required to function at a high level of effectiveness and alertness. But our predilection for activity goes beyond meeting our basic or even comfortable needs. If we are middle-class, we are likely to work longer hours than we have to in order to fulfil the requirements of our jobs – or than we have put in since workers were forced into punishing labour during the Industrial Revolution. Home life provides little relief: with perpetual access to the internet, maintaining one's health through exercise or attending to home improvements, it can be so busy that some sociologists have called it 'the third shift'. In a culture that constantly presents us with images of glamour and luxury, we are often caught up in the cult of The

Best: we want the best homes, best children, best vacations, best professional gigs. We think nothing of flying for twelve hours to a career-advancing meeting or a conference, the perils of jetlag notwithstanding. We absorb large quantities of culture, which may be all to the good; but too often, we consume culture in the spirit of – well, consumerism. We do things in order to have done them, or simply to fill time with activity. And of course we spend some hours each day on our digital devices, whether we need to or not.

Even children's schedules these days are filled up with extra lessons and other improving activities, and of course their young minds imbibe our underlying attitudes towards such things. Writing in the *New Yorker* a few years ago, the essayist Adam Gopnik describes his three-year-old daughter, who has invented an imaginary friend named Charlie Ravioli. She talks to him on her 'mobile phone' and wishes very much to see him. The only problem is that he is always too busy to play with her; he is otherwise engaged. Three-year-old Olivia is, of course, imitating the adults in her world, whose diaries are always full and who are always in a rush; in some way, she understands that the adults consider this condition to be somehow desirable.

We have good reasons to be busy. But I believe that if we fill our days with useful or useless tasks, it is because in our over-stimulated environments we have become addicted to activity – or what might be called hyperactivity – itself. The digital environment, with its endless supply of instant stimulation and gratification, ups the ante tremendously.

Hyperactivity is addictive partly because it can give us a sort of hedonic pleasure. It introduces a welcome sense of eventfulness and dynamism into our lives. Being in motion and on the go can seem both invigorating and gratifying. When we look through our friends' most recent postings on Facebook, or post a witty sentence on Twitter, we feel a small hit of pleasure. When we move from one appointment to another, from a power breakfast to a planning meeting in the office, we feel a sort of excitement about ourselves and our lives. When we drive ourselves to exhaustion by pushing ourselves to the limit of our energies, we may temporarily experience the kind of euphoria that marathon runners describe as 'runner's high'.

But after a while, incessant activity can leave us feeling depleted and oddly undernourished, as if the experiences we have been through have not taken root, or become part of ourselves. And, like

We get addicted to our devices . . . and to working on them after hours, sometimes in preference to human contact.

any hedonic habit, it can lead to states of mind which are not pleasurable at all. Digital addiction is the most recognized of hyperactive syndromes. In Korea and China there are 'detox camps' for addicted adolescents who appear to suffer terrible withdrawal symptoms as they attempt to stay unplugged. Elsewhere, there have been reports of virtual-world gamers dying from dehydration, as they are unable to leave their imaginary worlds for the ones in which their bodies exist. Dehydration is a serious condition, and a suggestive metaphor; compulsive fun turning into dangerous deprivation.

Digital technologies have introduced wondrous benefits into our lives and expanded our horizons; but they are a powerful double-edged force, whose impact on our emotions and minds can be potent. Even for someone of a boringly counter-addictive temperament like myself, digital seduction is hard to resist. For a while, I was seriously hooked on email, and had to give myself stern talks to stop checking it several times a day. I weaned myself from this habit by realizing that in being apparently busy in this way, I was actually doing nothing – in fact, wasting time doubly by disrupting my concentration, and distracting my attention from more compelling tasks. Now,

I understand that by contemporary standards, confining yourself to email in your virtual life may seem positively quaint; but even so, such compulsiveness can eventually turn quite unpleasant. On the affective level, digital cruising can quickly turn from excitement to anxiety, and then to a kind of disgust. It is no wonder that shifting among several media, or using them simultaneously, is called 'snacking'. As with snacking of a more literal kind, it can leave you feeling both bloated and unfilled.

Perhaps more worryingly, the consequences of hyperactivity – of trying to do too much at once – extend to a very concrete impact on the brain. We may feel, as we cook and text simultaneously, that our minds are quick and agile; but actually, the brain eventually becomes less efficient as we indulge in this, or other forms of multitasking. This is because the brain uses extra energy in switching from one task to another, and eventually it slows down and goes into a kind of gridlock. In the long term, the fragmentation of attention, a breaking up of focus and mental continuity, can disrupt neural connections in the brain and eventually lead to a literally 'shallower' neurological structure. It makes us – on the physiological level of the brain, as well as of the mind – less capable of concentration and continuous thought.

The psychological effects of hyperactivity on both young people and adults have also been closely studied, and not surprisingly, they include Hyperactive Attention Deficit Disorder – the diagnosis of choice for today's children – and the ubiquitous syndromes of anxiety and stress. Stress has been pronounced 'the greatest problem of the twenty-first century', and while such sound-bite alarms should be taken with a large grain of salt (the candidates for the century's greatest problem are many), there is no doubt that in our relatively comfortable society, perhaps even more than elsewhere, stress is a ubiquitous condition.

On a deeper level, psychoanalysts have noted a great rise in patients who suffer from Borderline Personality Disorder – a condition in which a person moves from one 'high' experience to another, without being able to put them together, or create any sense of internal continuity or coherent story about themselves – what is sometimes called 'the narrative self'. Such fragmentation of internal life can be very distressing; and borderline patients are typically addicted to alcohol, drugs or shopping.

Most of us don't suffer from such extreme disturbances; but we may feel that hopping from one small gratification to another, or being dispersed among several tasks at once, means that our experiences are not only fragmented, but somehow temporary and thin. It leaves us anxious and dissatisfied.

My friend Emma, who works in an interesting international job, says with some passion that the lack of time for focused reflection is 'the central problem' she feels in her life. It undermines her sense that she can either take pleasure in what she is doing, or accomplish anything worthwhile or meaningful. Emma struggles with how to manage this, and sometimes longs to be back at university, where you occasionally have the luxury of thinking about 'one thing at a time'.

The seminal philosophers of ancient Greece – Epicurus, Socrates, Aristotle – thought of their endeavour not as an abstract process of reasoning, but as a therapy of the soul, and whatever their disagreements, they were unanimous on certain basic principles of well-being. Momentary pleasures of hedonism are distinct from deeper and more lasting satisfaction; and in order to achieve such satisfaction, we need to reflect on who we are and what our lives are for. We cannot be fully human without thinking about what being human means.

Our forms of momentary self-indulgence are many, but it is hyperactivity which is our favoured as well as most pervasive form of hedonism; and by its very nature, it is a form of gratification which undermines reflection – and well-being – of a deeper or more sustained kind. Emma struggles with this problem; and I think all of us need to consider how to give ourselves time for focused thought and calm concentration; and how to recover the richness of our inner as well as our external lives.

2. Challenges of Choice

On the way home from work, you stop off at a popular chain store featuring rather inexpensive knock-off fashions. Half an hour later, having looked and tried on clothes in a sort of daze, you emerge with some tops in the latest colours and yet another scarf to add to your collection. Do you actually need them? Well, you think rather sheepishly, perhaps you'll find a use for them later; maybe they'll somehow change the way you look and think of yourself this summer. As you walk on, you think you should visit your mother, who has been feeling unwell; but you've been invited to a party at which who knows what may happen, or whom you may meet. You're torn; you really don't know what you should, or would actually prefer, to do.

For Emma, as for many of us, the problems of excessive busyness are compounded by the constant need to make choices and decisions, in matters ranging from frivolous to important, from material to moral. The sheer plenitude of material goods available to us – from food to fashion, ingenious home appliances to sexy cars – can itself result in forms of compulsive behaviour, as we can see in occasional outbreaks of mass consumer hysteria, in which people have been trampled by crowds pressing into shopping outlets when some big sale is announced. I must say that my memories of the old Eastern Europe, where only two kinds of shampoo and three colours of house paint were available at the best of times, occasionally acquire a certain idyllic tinge.

But in our advanced, multicultural democracies, the freedom – or is it the necessity – of choice extends to more essential and existential issues. On every level of our lives, from childbirth to death, from education to religion, from career to sexual identity, we are free to do as we like and to change our minds as often as we wish. Of course, the idea that we are totally free to choose is to some extent an illusion, as many commentators, including Renata Salecl in her insightful book *The Tyranny of Choice*, have pointed out. The range of our actual choices is limited by our circumstances, abilities and actual opportunities. I might wish I could be a wonderful ballerina, or buy that bottle-green Jaguar, but I can't.

Sometimes you can have too much of a good thing – and much too much choice.

Nevertheless, because we are presented with ostensible options in all areas of life, we have a nagging sense that maybe we should be taking advantage of them. Even if we don't want to break up with our current partner, we think that we could just perhaps find – or at least look for – others. After all, they are right out there in large numbers, on all those dating websites. Even if we are not about to leave our job, it is hard to get rid of a murmur in our head saying that we could find something more interesting, or more worthwhile, or better paid. We see other people doing something different or seemingly more gratifying all the time, both within our immediate vicinity, and in the larger world made visible to us by the old and new media. At the same time, the great diversity of lifestyles, options and values in our cultures and open societies means that there are few common criteria for making important life choices. How do you decide if it's better to be more successful, or more devoted to the welfare of others? How do you ascertain if you prefer to be monogamous, or insouciantly serial in your relationships? At each level of our experience, we need to find motives and reasons for what we want or don't want to do, within ourselves. At the same time, the sheer seductions of availability make it hard for us to decide among various options, and to separate external influences from our own values and preferences. Our minds are overcrowded in these less tangible ways as well, and this sometimes leads to a kind of stoppage, or the inability to make any decisions at all.

The same philosophers who made distinctions between momentary hedonism and deeper satisfaction thought that no matter what material comforts or refinements we enjoy, we cannot attain the good life without some idea of shaping purpose, or conviction of meaningfulness and worth, pervading our moments and activities. That is a grand goal and aspiration; but even on a less overarching scale, the plenitude of choice on every level makes finding a direction and ascertaining our own aims more difficult.

How then, given the pressures and distractions of our lives, can we regain our perspective and coherence of self? How can we reclaim a sense that our experiences have personal meaning and depth – that we are not moving through them routinely or shallowly? The pressures are real and not easily dispelled; and one kind of solution is to opt out of them altogether, and adopt various forms of 'dropping out': living in an isolated place, forsaking the idea of a regular job, or going off to a remote Zen monastery. Yet others declare a boycott on choice itself, taking an example from such books as *Choosing Not to Choose* by the legal scholar Cass Sunstein. I do not mean to dismiss such solutions; for some people, they are right and make for happier lives. But for most of us, these are extreme measures. Unless we are of a particularly meditative or solitary temperament, most of us want to live in the world and remain engaged with it. We want to be effective in what we do, to lead sociable lives and cultivate close relationships and friendships. We want, sometimes, to take risks, stretch ourselves further or have adventures.

The question for most of us is not how to retreat from the world, but how to retain our bearings within it, and to live more fully rather than just more busily. The temperate answer I want to propose is that we need to alternate periods of energetic activity with relaxed receptivity, directed effort with intervals of goal-less, undutiful leisure. Whether we have seen the neurological evidence or not, many of us sense the need for time free of distractions, and the deprivation that follows from its lack. It is easy, amidst the plethora of diversions and options offered by our societies, to lose track of why we do what we do, what we truly want, and what it is about our activities or our lives that we value and love. In order to discern or rediscover our own, internally impelled values and motives, we need to pull back from driven activity, and to take time to process and make sense of our experiences; to delve into the deeper strata of our inner lives, or to examine our situations through more analytic thought. We also need moments of unpressured idleness to replenish our energies and restore our capacity for ordinary pleasure and enjoyment. If we don't take the time to do that, we can become depleted and disoriented, and begin to move through what we are doing automatically, without a conscious sense of purpose, or making real acts of choice. And that, eventually, makes us not only less satisfied, but less effective at what we do.

To put it simply, I want to remind us of what the early philosophers understood so well: the value and salutary power of reflection and self-knowledge. These are worth developing for their own sake; but I believe they are also necessary if we are to replace the excitement of hectic and sometimes aimless activity with full consciousness and purposeful engagement. True engagement – the ability to give ourselves deliberately and unreservedly to a task or a personal interaction – arises from a clear sense of our own desires, goals and intentions. It is when our energies and our perspective are replenished that we can return to our active lives with a renewed sense of pleasure and commitment. In other words, it is only if we periodically disengage, that we can become truly and effectively engaged.

This book has a tripartite structure: in the first part, I have tried to set out the problems of hyperactivity and excessive choice, and the states of mind they produce. In the second, I will consider the pleasures and uses of leisure, and mention some of my favourite ways to be idle, in the hope that they'll stimulate some of your own ideas on the subject. These include not only passive relaxation, but cultivating all our capacities for curiosity, appreciation of beauty and creative contemplation – acts and states of self which nurture us and allow us to perceive the world more fully. In the third part I will look at the experience of happy absorption or 'flow' that follows from purposeful engagement, and its various expressions in work, relationships and creative play.

I have written about some of the problems of fast and slow temporality in my short book on Time. But the questions raised there have continued to preoccupy me, and here I would like to ex-

plore them from a different point of view, and to
look not only at the patterns of human temporality, but how we can create ways of moving through
time which are meaningful and enriching. A richness of experience proceeds from within and is
intimately bound up with ways of understanding
ourselves and our situation. I want to explore
some of these connections, and to suggest that being fully and consciously involved in our lives is
the only reliable antidote to the discomforts of
ennui or anxious emptiness; and that for that, we
need sometimes to take time off and time out.

II. Leisure

3. Idleness

Why do many of us find it so difficult to take time off from obligations, or uninterrupted activity – to allow ourselves, occasionally, to do nothing?

In 1952, an American psychiatrist, Alexander Reid Martin, wrote an article titled 'The Fear of Relaxation and Leisure'. In it, he describes patients who could not tolerate the idea of time free from work. Some of them could not go on holiday without a doctor's prescription; others had heart attacks or committed suicide when they forced themselves, or were forced, to take a vacation.

Not many people have such extreme reactions to going on holiday anymore; instead, to some extent we have banished real leisure altogether. Our restlessness, and the appurtenances of digital activity, can be taken anywhere; and many of us bring them with us on our vacations. It seems that while we are no longer driven by the work ethic, as Dr Martin's patients were, an addiction to activity – and an accompanying fear of restfulness – is still with us. We may hold to the subliminal belief that occupation – of whatever kind – is virtuous, and laziness a vice. Or we may be afraid of falling into a Kierkegaardian state of emptiness, or what in early Christianity was called sloth – a vice leading straight to the ultimate sin of despair.

The word 'leisure' comes from Latin *licere*, to be permitted – and perhaps the first step in learning how to take time off is to give ourselves permission to do so. We might think of those early philosophers who devoted their lives to the cultivation of the self, and to conversation about the essential matters of existence, through which they thought they could also improve the lives of others. Or we might remember the thinkers of many periods who saw leisure as the very foundation of culture: of contemplation, the spiritual life and even the liberal arts. (The Greek word for school – *schole* – was derived from the word for leisure.) No less a personage than Bertrand Russell, in an essay called 'In Praise of Idleness', averred 'that . . . there is far too much work done in the world, that immense harm is caused by the belief that work is virtuous, and that what needs to be preached in modern industrial countries is quite different from what always has been preached'. Russell, like his friend John Maynard Keynes, thought the solution was to adopt a four-hour working day, which would leave everyone free to pursue philosophy, cultural diversions and adult learning.

I'm not sure that the majority of humankind would find that much free time a boon, or that these oddly unrealistic proposals would be economically tenable for any society. Probably none of the older models of leisure are suited to our situation; for one thing, we are no longer divided between leisured and labouring classes, with free time being the prerogative of aristocratic elites. The great majority of us need to work, although perhaps not as relentlessly as many of us choose to; and we need to find ways of being leisurely that fit into our lives and enrich them. Still, the value attached to leisure in various traditions should reassure us. It is also worth remembering that leisure is not the same as laziness; and that it is necessary not only to the life of the mind, but to our physical and emotional well-being.

If we have given ourselves the assent to take time off, then perhaps we can first of all learn to enjoy moments or hours of unscripted idleness – intervals in which we can slough off the tensions accumulated during the day or week, and return to more pleasurable states of self and mind. Our cultures provide structured ways of calming down, such as yoga or the very popular Mindfulness movement, which specializes in condensed, short-term meditation. Indeed, the very brevity of Mindfulness sessions acknowledges the busy conditions of our lives; and its programme teaches its followers techniques for clearing their minds and reviving their energies through a foreshortened and compressed meditational process. Recently, some big organizations (such as Google) have caught on to the usefulness of such breaks – just as some of them have built in short naps for their employees – in making people work more efficiently afterwards. Many Mindfulness adherents have testified to the beneficial effects of such techniques, and there is no reason to doubt them. Others, however, find it too regimented and didactic; and I must admit that the idea of napping or meditating on cue in order to work better in the afternoon fills me with slight dread. It also seems to me a contradictory method of becoming peacefully self-aware.

My preference is for forms of relaxation which are less programmatic and more improvised; which proceed from individual personality rather than generalized precepts; and which restore us to a sense of positive pleasure in the texture of our daily lives, rather than just clearing our minds of problematic thoughts. It would be rather ironic for me to give instructions on how to do this; but perhaps some examples can be suggestive. I have a friend who sets aside a day a week to do nothing that she doesn't feel like doing, and to follow her impulses if she does feel like doing something. She often sits in her favourite spot along an urban river, or in a cafe; sometimes she finds herself writing in her diary. A composer I know told me that he spends a part of each morning sitting at his kitchen table with a cup of coffee and letting thoughts and sensations arise as they will, without imposing particular order or meaning on them. He is a productive artist who understands the need for disciplined work; but he says that his seemingly lazy mornings are important to his process of composition.

Not all of us are going to write musical works as a result of a slow morning; but we all occasionally need to be able simply to savour the moment, to follow our errant musings and impulses, and sense the rhythms and inclinations of our thoughts and bodies. One consequence of spending so much time in the virtual world is that we become disconnected from our own physical presence and the physicality of our environment. Aside from depriving us of a fundamental sense of pleasure, this can affect our well-being. After all, the body is the very basis of the self; if it becomes too abstracted or dissociated from us, we may lose track of its needs, or the relish of its appetites. We may not know, for example, how much, or how little, we actually want to eat.

Savouring a long cup of coffee; relishing a new recipe that appeals to us; taking a slow saunter in a park or down an urban street without forcing the pace of our walk; these are ways of reconnecting with the sensuality of our bodies when we are not straining them through exercise or restraining them by sitting at the desk. They are ways of savouring the small pleasures of daily life, and of recovering the basic enjoyment of moving through the physical world.

Walking is of course a pastime with a long tradition, and writers from Coleridge to William Hazlitt have testified to the connection between the rhythms of this basic activity and creative thought. Coleridge especially took heroic walks, roaming for tens of miles over hill and dale, often in adverse weather conditions. On our idle days, we might not want to do anything so strenuous, and might want instead to amble in our own neighbourhood. If we live near a park, or in a rural setting, we can get the benefits of natural surroundings. Natural beauty, if we can relax into it, is a source of never-ending variety and aesthetic pleasure. Moreover, studies have shown that it has undoubted positive effects on our health. For example, hospital patients whose rooms look out onto a garden or some trees recover faster than those who have to stare all day at monotonous concrete.

But urban walking also has its rich sensations. Exploring one's own neighbourhood can be as satisfying as travelling to exotic places, in a different way. When we walk down a familiar street which perhaps leads to something surprising, we can notice not only the large panorama, but the specific details. A new shop or an interesting bit of architectural design we've never spotted can also enliven our interest in our surroundings, and aesthetic appreciation. We are attached to our environment through our connection to small things as well as abstractions or big vistas – through what anthropologists, and latterly airport advertisements, call local knowledge.

Here's Virginia Woolf on taking an evening walk in London, in an essay called 'Street Haunting':

Passing, glimpsing, everything seems accidentally but miraculously sprinkled with

A Sunday Afternoon on the Island of La Grande Jatte –
an image of civilized (and civilizing) leisure.

beauty, as if the tide of trade which deposits its burden so punctually and prosaically upon the shores of Oxford Street had this night cast up nothing but treasure. With no thought of buying, the eye is sportive and generous; it creates; it adorns; it enhances.

Observing what is around us and registering errant impressions is a state not so much of passive inaction as of alert receptivity. Allowing ourselves to notice, to be open to our surroundings, is a way of awakening our curiosity in the world outside ourselves. The philosophical school of phenomenology was based on the idea that knowledge is derived from sensory perception. Such perception is a primary state of consciousness; but even so, it is highly complex. In order to perceive anything – to see the room we are in as a room, for example – the brain has to coordinate several neuronal strands: visual, auditory, spatial. How that is done – how such coordination adds up to instant and seamless perception – is still one of the central mysteries of conscious awarenesss.

But we do know that the brain changes throughout our lives, and is modified by external experience. It is through registering impressions of our surroundings that we add to the storehouse of our internal experience – the imagery we carry within ourselves, but also our memories.

We are, first of all, sentient creatures. Our primary perceptions and impressions are part of what we are; but in order to be open to such impressions, we need sometimes to slow down, and turn our attention outwards – to look. When we are rushing to the tube, we don't really see the people we are passing, or, say, a new flower stand. Of course, sometimes (or rather, often) we need to rush to the tube. But we also need times of unstrained idleness in which we can meander spontaneously, and be alert and curious about our surroundings. This is a way of enriching our repertory of memories and textures of perception, and of reminding ourselves that there is pleasure in being sentient and alive.

4. Introspection

Improvised, unstructured idleness can return us to our sensual, sentient selves; it can revive a sense of enjoyment in our bodily, physical existence, and reawaken our receptivity to our surroundings.

But aside from having a physical existence and perceptions, we also have what we have come to call the psyche (which is simply the Greek word for the soul) – that complex and often turbulent realm of thoughts and emotions, sub-verbal tensions and subterranean sensations which is the very material of our selves. If we are not to lose track of who we are or what we want, we need occasionally to look into that realm and examine what we find there; to catch up on what has happened to us in the last week or month, and how we feel about it; to sense the conflicts or tensions which may have accumulated while we have been absorbed in daily activity, and try to understand where they come from, and what they mean to us. In other words, we need to give some time not only to idle rumination, but to more strenuous self-investigation and introspection – to the cultivation of self-knowledge.

Why is it important to do so? On one level, self-knowledge is a self-evident good, one of the foundations of philosophy and the hallmarks of civilization. The capacity not only to exist, but to understand ourselves, is what makes us fully human, rather than purely animal or biological beings. The motto 'Know thyself' was apparently one of the Delphic maxims inscribed in the Temple of Apollo; its origins were ascribed to any number of early philosophers, and Plato has Socrates use it as one of the central injunctions in his Dialogues. For as long as we have been conscious beings, we have tried to understand who we are, how to live the good life, and where we fit into the larger scheme of things – the known world around us, and the universe which remained for much of history almost entirely unknown. And, from early on, cultures and religions developed various techniques and practices of self-examination. Socrates tried to further knowledge and self-knowledge through dynamic dialogue – asking his interlocutors questions about such matters as love, or friendship, or the nature of politics, and encouraging them to press their questioning further, until they understood the very essence and the widest implications of the subjects or problems they were examining. Buddhist meditation developed the practice of sitting still for prolonged periods of time and impartially observing what is happening within us – a technique which, in its Western versions, is once again becoming popular in contemporary cultures. Other religions have asked us to examine our souls in the light of received laws or ideas of sin and salvation.

But I also want to suggest that if we need to look inwards – to keep 'in touch' with ourselves, as our contemporary phrase has it – that is not only because self-knowledge is a virtue, but because its lack diminishes us, and makes us anxious and unhappy. It also – quite crucially – prevents us from orienting ourselves in the world, or making well-founded choices, or knowing what we believe or want. Lack of self-knowledge leaves us, internally, in the dark.

Mind you, if you consider it for a moment, the very need for deliberate cultivation and attainment of self-understanding can be baffling. Unless we want to study ourselves as physical or biological objects (an important, but not a reflective form of investigation), how can we *not* know ourselves? How can the thing that is ourselves be opaque or mysterious to the thing we are? And indeed, on one level, self-knowledge is a natural property of our minds, and an aspect of consciousness which is built into the structure of our brains – that is, self-consciousness. We are the only species endowed with this faculty; that is, the ability not only to see or know something – to spot a bird, say, or learn a new song – but to know that we see and know it. And, even as we experience various states of self – say, anger or sadness – we know that we are experiencing them. In a sense, we are observing ourselves all the time.

But on another level, understanding ourselves is not easy or automatic at all. We know that sometimes we are perplexed by very basic questions: what exactly are we up to in our lives, what are our actual desires and aspirations? Are we happy with what we are doing, or do we want, somehow, to change? And we have probably all had moments in which we say awkward things we didn't mean to utter; or times when we have been overwhelmed by feelings – anger, shame, or for that matter, love – we didn't exactly know we had; or periods during which, say, we drink too much, without exactly wanting or choosing to. Some of us may have experienced not only confusing feelings and impulses, but moments of deeper disorientation. If we rush ceaselessly through disconnected activities without checking in on our moods or motives, we can lose track of ourselves; in a sense, we lose the ability to experience our experiences. A rather high-flying friend, Peter, tells me that he went through a period – after several months of working, playing and travelling ceaselessly – when he simply didn't remember where and who he was when he woke up. Such states are, of course, very disconcerting, and he had to take some time off work in order to regain his bearings and his sense of his normal, grounded identity.

It seems that in the realm of our inner life, self-knowledge is not a given of our nature, nor easily attained. The practice of self-reflection needs to be developed and nurtured – and in our age of virtual hyperactivity, this does not come to us easily or naturally. Our very notions of what it means to know ourselves – or to have an identity – are being fundamentally altered by digital technologies. In our abbreviated digital communications (whether on Twitter or on Facebook), we present and express the most transitory and superficial aspects of our personalities. We report what we are doing at a particular moment; or give sound-bite versions of an idea or opinion ('I am driving down horrible M21 and hoping to reach Villesville soon'; 'That was a great speech at the climate change conference'). We 'know' ourselves through the selfies we take of ourselves, and which give us back the visual surfaces of our activities and selves. This can undoubtedly be fun, and images can function as a memory-aid – they can remind us where we've been, and what we have done. But such reminders of surface impressions are not an equivalent of knowing ourselves in three dimensions; indeed, our addiction to recording our experiences moment by moment may deflect us from our immediate responses and sensations, and prevent us from experiencing the moment in its non-virtual actuality in the first place. (And, incidentally, images can lie very well. In a selfie taken in front of some Greek taverna, we may be smiling toothsomely to indicate we're having a great time; but in fact, we may be in the middle of an upsetting conflict with our partner, and in a terrible mood.) What we are in danger of losing in our predilection for producing and conveying instantaneous information is the very idea of inwardness, and of understanding ourselves not only in the immediate moment, but through extended time. Accessing that 'deep space' of our internal lives requires a more sustained process of introspection.

How, then, can we develop the capacity – and the subtle skills – of looking inwards? How can we begin to delve into and explore the aspects of ourselves which are not easily reachable, or known? It is of course impossible to be prescriptive about this most individual and delicate of endeavours; but the first step is certainly to turn off our smartphone, and find a place which is free from external distractions, and which allows us to retreat temporarily to the privacy of our thoughts and feelings.

Of course, this may be, to many of us, a discomfiting prospect. When we speak about 'threats to privacy', what we usually mean are the dangers of government or corporate access to our computerized information. But in the meantime, we are all too often willing to give away the most meaningful kind of privacy – the privacy of our personal and internal experience. In sending intimate disclosures to dozens or hundreds of 'friends' in our network, or 'sharing' images of ourselves in various states of dress or undress, we lose the habit, or the ability, to contain our experiences within ourselves and come to understand them from within.

The silence of quiet rumination can seem to us to be a state of frightening emptiness and stasis.

But self-reflection is hardly equivalent to blankness or cessation of effort. It requires focus and a particular kind of concentration. It also requires intervals of time for the very different kind of temporality which courses within ourselves – within subjectivity. Internal time does not move in chronological progressions. A thought can arise and develop over an extended period; a glide from the present to the past can happen in a split second. Looking inwards is not a process that can be rushed, or in which we can try to be efficient.

One experiment in what might be called informal self-analysis has been described in two charming books by the writer and painter Marion Milner, who eventually became a psychoanalyst, and who wrote under the pseudonym Joanna Field. In *A Life of One's Own* and *An Experiment in Leisure*, she tells us that she wants to overcome a sense of confusion in her life, and to discover what really makes her happy or gives her enjoyment. She does so by exploring 'the no-man's land which lay between the dark kingdom of the psychoanalyst and the cultivated domain of my conscious thought . . . I had not realized that by a few simple tricks of observation I could become aware of quite unexpected things in myself.'

One of these tricks was to keep herself 'particularly alert to any little movements going on in the back of my mind, passing ideas which were often quite irrelevant to my task of the moment . . . I called these "butterflies" for they silently fluttered in from nowhere and were gone in a moment.'

Sometimes, as Marion Milner discovered, acknowledging such 'passing ideas' requires the courage of honesty – of facing up to something which may seem incompatible with our self-image, or with what we think should matter to us. In *A Life of One's Own* she describes a long reverie, in which she tried to discern what was making her distressed on a particular morning; as she sits on a river bank and allows the rhythm of the flowing water to encourage her own flow of thoughts, she eventually admits to herself that what nags at the back of her mind is an earlier moment when she failed, in conversation with a man she found interesting, to hold his attention. A small admission, seemingly, but one which was difficult for her to make and which gave her great relief once it was made. She could go on to savour

the beauty of her surroundings, and enjoy the
morning fully without being distracted by an obscure internal discomfort.

Marion Milner went on to study psychoanalysis. But whether we are aware of psychoanalytic
theory or not, in our contemporary cultures, it is
psychoanalysis, with its many associated thera-
pies, which provides the main model for understanding ourselves in depth, and for the practice
of introspection. Psychoanalysis is the discipline
that in the last century and a half has given us
the most systematic and probing observations of
internal life, and the most comprehensive model of
the self and its development. Indeed, psychoanalytic theory can be seen as a modern updating of
the long philosophic lineage – a philosophy which
adds to the older templates of human nature the
element of deep subjectivity. Within the psychoanalytic conception of the self, the 'irrational' aspects of our make-up – violent emotions, instincts,
inchoate impulses, the unconscious – are seen not
as something to be vanquished by the light of rationality, but as basic materials of human identity
which have to be taken into account in our understanding of ourselves, and which are a source of
significant knowledge and self-knowledge.

Such assumptions have come to constitute for

us, to quote W. H. Auden on Freud, 'the climate of opinion'. Psychoanalysis has given us the terms through which to understand ourselves, and sometimes the lenses through which to view the world. (The Italian filmmaker Bernardo Bertolucci once said, 'I have a third lens in my camera; it's not Kodak or Zeiss – it's Freud.') As we embark on the project of self-examination, it might be useful to keep some of the insights and techniques of depth-therapies in mind – although we certainly don't need to be theoretical about ourselves, or to think through a theoretical vocabulary. We might, initially, give ourselves over to the state which Milner discovered for herself, and which therapists call reverie or free association: a kind of non-judgemental attention in which we allow images, memories or indiscriminate associations to float to the surface of our minds, and stop ourselves from fending them off, no matter how insignificant they may seem. We need, in a way, to be open to ourselves and to what we discover within – and to discover it in our own words and ways.

What we find there will undoubtedly be very specific, and perhaps surprising even to ourselves. When I was studying psychoanalysis, I was struck by the great variety and singularity of people's inner lives. I remember, for example, a woman who could not fall asleep when the street outside was quiet, because the noises of life reassured her that she would not disappear while she slept; that there was something to come back to. There was a young man who worried perennially that he was not thankful enough to people he met; or that he was too stickily thankful. The patterns of psychic life are difficult to generalize; and perhaps the first step in self-examination is to acknowledge those small ways of acting or reacting which are a part of our particular personalities; to notice, for example, when we are pretending to enjoy ourselves at a party without actually doing so, or when we are bothered by a seemingly insignificant exchange with a colleague (did her lip curl in slight scorn, even as she was forcing herself to be respectful about a proposal we made?) and to be honest about why that is.

It is the distinguishing hallmark of psychoanalysis that – unlike other theories of self – it takes such individual traits and quirks seriously. In contrast to traditional philosophies which have seen human nature in the light of general precepts, psychoanalysis started with close observation of particular people, and the often unpredictable patterns and details of their interior lives – and within its picture of the self, such details matter. Our emotions, thoughts, inner conflicts and passions are the essence of what makes us human – and our particular passions and stories are what make us the specific individuals we are.

This is also in interesting contrast to Buddhist meditation, which, in its more extended forms (as opposed to the meditation-lite offered in Mindfulness programmes) provides another model for self-reflection, and one which has often been compared to psychoanalysis. There are indeed affinities between the two practices; but the crucial difference, it seems to me, is in their attitudes to the character of the individual personality and self. Buddhist meditation proceeds from the premise that the world as we know it – the world of appearances – is ultimately meaningless and veils a more permanent reality; and that the individual self (which, after all, will be reincarnated as something else after death) is essentially insignificant. Nor are the contents of our inner lives – thoughts, feelings, fantasies – of much importance. In meditational sessions, people are instructed to remember that 'thoughts are only thoughts; fantasies are only fantasies' – and to let them go as if they were cloudy vapour. The aim (at least as it is conveyed in Western versions of meditational philosophy) is to clear our minds of both, and to sense the ephemeral nature of our concerns – a state which allows for truer and clearer perception of reality. Why worry about that colleague's curled lip, if we are an ephemeral speck within a transient and ultimately illusory reality?

There have been eloquent testimonies to the power of meditation, although these usually come from adherents who have retreated for prolonged periods to ashrams or monasteries, or other places devoted exclusively to meditative practices – who have, in other words, made it a way of life. But others have found that while meditation helps them in sloughing off temporary tensions, it does not address or resolve the actual conflicts or stresses which accumulate so easily in our societies – however small they may seem in the larger scheme of things.

Of course worrying about someone's ambiguous gesture of disapproval can be overdone. But if such things nag at us, if an errant expression surfaces with a disturbing clarity before we go to sleep, that may be because for us it may have significance, and hold clues to some deeper, or more important concerns – say, an excessive fear of rejection, or a sense of one's own inadequacy. Within the psychoanalytic conception of the self, such oddities of feeling and quirks of personality are seen as important; and the aim is not to dispel them by declaring their insignificance, but to address them and understand them in all their dimensions. In formal depth-therapy, a small symptom (repeatedly forgetting the keys to one's apartment, say) or an odd reaction which has assumed a disproportionate importance in the account of a person's week (the patient was annoyed rather than sympathetic to a friend who was ill) is pursued through associations, or inter-pretation, to what may be their deeper or un-acknowledged sources in the patient's psychic life – so that eventually, the underlying causes of surface difficulties can hopefully be grasped and resolved.

At the same time, psychoanalysis offers power-ful suggestions as to why self-knowledge is so difficult to attain. This is not because we are in-sufficiently clever or incapable of rigorous ratioci-native thought about the world; or because we live in a perceptual cave, where true reality is veiled from our eyes. Rather, it is because we ourselves are hidden from ourselves; because some of the forces which drive us and impel our sensations and feelings are not fully known to us. They are, in fact, unconscious.

In Freud's first formulations, parts of our internal life become inaccessible to us because of the mechanisms of repression – because certain feelings or impulses (in his hypothesis, these were mostly sexual) are so intolerable in some circumstances that they have to be 'forgotten', or hidden out of consciousness. Freud's first patients suffered from such florid symptoms as paralysis without any physiological cause, or the inability to speak in one's native language, or coughing unstoppably when certain subjects or memories were touched on. The work of psychoanalysis was to help patients bring the repressed feelings masked by such symptoms to the surface – to become conscious of them; and this was often a very painful process.

The lack of self-knowledge, on this level, can lead to illness and emotional paralysis; and sometimes to wasted lives. The effort of self-knowledge is not only ennobling, but necessary to our happiness and health. In our time, as many contemporary psychoanalysts have noted, the failure to understand what is going on within ourselves is likely to come not from repression, but from the scattering and fragmentation of our internal

Freud's couch – an icon of psychoanalysis, and of deep
self-investigation.

lives – the inability to figure out the connections between our disparate activities, or even to remember them, or to give them personal meaning. This of course mirrors the fragmentation of our external lives, and is greatly exacerbated by digital technologies and the scattering of attention – of mind and feeling – they encourage.

None of this is an argument for studying psychoanalysis or entering formal psychotherapy; but it makes the need for periods of self-examination more urgent. If we want to avoid states of stress or disorientation so easily induced by our lifestyles, we need to gather the fragments of our experience together, and to make sense of their meanings to us – perhaps before passing problems or worries become more deeply and perplexingly embedded in our emotional lives, and turn into more distressing states of inner disorientation or mysterious anxiety. What do we feel – and think – about what has happened to us during the previous week or month? Why does a particular incident we didn't have time to think about continue to worry us? What does it touch off in ourselves that gives it importance out of its actual proportion? In order to track down the significance of such details to their sources in ourselves, we may need to move from states of reverie to a more strenuous exploration of our inner lives.

Insight can catch us unawares in almost any situation – as we are taking a bath, or boarding a bus – and such small epiphanies can constitute clues to our particular predispositions and personalities. But aside from passing perceptions or sensations, our inner lives are also affected by pressures or conflicts which are more deeply and more stubbornly embedded in the structure of our subjectivity. In order to understand those, we need not only to be receptive to the errant impressions or associations which surface from our minds, but to think about them in a more focused and concentrated way. By 'thinking' here, I do not mean the activity of abstract reasoning; but rather, a process that absorbs the whole self, and that takes into account those elusive entities called emotions as well as impersonal or broader ideas. Contemporary psychoanalysts refer to 'the space to think' – a non-chartable terrain which includes all of our affective and ratiocinative capacities – and it is that elusive but crucial territory that we need both to open up and to traverse if we want to become conscious of what is going on within us. We need to think inwards, and to think from within.

What we discover through such explorations may be, initially, quite disconcerting. The deep space of subjectivity can be a turbulent realm, full of feelings we would rather not have – anger, shame, guilt, envy, vulnerability, dread of death – and that we are loath to acknowledge. But such acknowledgement can bring great relief: the relief of clarity. If we understand our proclivities to anger, say, we may not succumb so easily to irrational fits of fury, ostensibly provoked by small daily conflicts (or because someone snatched our taxi or parking space) but actually fuelled by, say, feeling inadequately appreciated or loved; we may not be overtaken by an onset of sudden anxiety on the way from a meeting, which actually masks a sense of sadness and loss of safety caused by a close person's death. We may be less in the dark.

Here is Marion Milner again, as she progressed further in her experiment in self-knowledge: 'And it was gradually, by exploring this region,' she writes, referring to something like subjective space, 'that I came to understand what forces were distorting and limiting my powers of perception, preventing me from making constant use of that source of happiness which my earlier observations had brought to light.'

Emma, who has made a habit of making 'the

space to think' in her life in order to counter the sense of being perpetually scattered, has found that systematic introspection can make her better acquainted with the distorting forces in herself, and lead her to salutary insight. 'After a while, I can see what's being played out,' she says. 'Or what I'm playing out.' For example, after examining some very odd reactions to her friends and colleagues, she began to realize how envious she was of many of her professional and even personal contacts. Emma is a highly ethical person; and she doesn't believe that professional success, or high salaries, or a friend's attractiveness, are important enough to warrant envy. And yet, she had to admit that envy was what she felt, and that it was a troubling sensation – partly because it was so dissonant with her self-image and values. It was only after she confronted this sensation head-on and circled around its causes (her own dissatisfaction with herself; her father's early preference for her younger sibling) that this complex feeling began to lift. Although the process of arriving at this realization was difficult, there was great pleasure for her in reaching new and deeper understanding – as well as in gaining control over troubling emotions. Understanding is its own reward; when Emma reached it, she found she went to work in a happier mood, and stopped being unnecessarily suspicious of her occasionally more successful colleagues. As an incidental bonus, this made her a nicer and more effective colleague herself, and led to a small promotion. Inner conflict can hamper us greatly, and its resolutions can open up unexpected vistas.

Indeed, arriving at new levels of understanding is, I think, one of the great underestimated pleasures of our mental life. Remaining at the surface of our experience can make us feel scattered and trivial; delving down and becoming conscious of what is within can give us a sense of clarity and internal enlargement – an almost literal deepening of perception. It also means we are less at the mercy of obscure emotions, and can draw on our inner energies more directly.

Freud's formulation for this kind of self-discovery was, 'Where id was, there shall ego be.' A more contemporary formulation of a similar idea comes, perhaps surprisingly, from the life sciences, especially neuroscience – the field in which the nature of consciousness and emotions is investigated not only speculatively, but through microscopic probes into the body and brain. On one level, students of evolutionary biology have identified several 'universal emotions' – fear, anger, sadness, happiness, disgust and surprise – which are the body's instinctive reactions to the realities we encounter in our environment (danger stimulates fear, rotten meat disgust, etc.). But cutting-edge research in neuroscience suggests that the more subtle and specific feelings we experience are created by a feedback loop between body and brain; that is, between our physiological reactions and that still mysterious entity called consciousness. Here is Antonio Damasio, a leading neuroscientist with a distinctly philosophical bent, on the processes which go into the making of emotion:

> Body and brain are engaged in a continuous interactive dance. Thoughts implemented in the brain can induce emotional states that are implemented in the body, while the body can change the brain's landscape and thus the substrate for thoughts. The brain states, which correspond to certain mental states, cause particular body states to occur; body states are then mapped in the brain and incorporated into the ongoing mental states. A small

alteration on the brain side of the system can have major consequences for the body state (think of the release of any hormone); likewise, a small change on the body side (think of a broken tooth filling) can have a major effect on the mind once the change is mapped and perceived as acute pain.

This is important, in part because it confirms with empirical precision what our experience so often tells us: that our minds are not disconnected from our moods, and that what we think is an intrinsic part of how we feel – and vice versa. Emotions are not only physiological currents of bad or good sensation that rise up within our bodies; they have meanings, and they proceed from the meanings we give to our experience. Indeed, the ability – and the need – to endow our experiences with significance is what makes us deeply human. In his book *Man's Search for Meaning*, Viktor Frankl, an existential psychoanalyst who was also a concentration camp survivor, suggests that even great suffering can be borne if we understand its meanings. On the other hand, even small doses of stress or unhappiness can drive us to antidepressants if we move through such states in a fog of disorientation.

In a way, the two leading modern theories of self – psychoanalysis and neuroscience – have gone some way to heal the split (which has never existed in our experience, but was inscribed into our 'rationalist' traditions of belief and thought) between irrational impulse and the 'higher faculties' of rational thought, or between body and mind. Both contemporary models of consciousness tell us that meaningful self-knowledge is knowledge that proceeds from our whole selves, and takes the whole self into account. In order to understand we need not only to think, but to think feelingly.

Introspective Memory

It is important to make sense of our experience in the present; but if we are not to risk another kind of fragmentation, we need to traverse 'the space to think' not only through its emotional strata but through layers of time. In our hyperactive lives, and particularly in our transactions with digital technologies, our experiences are all too often curtailed to the abbreviated moment – the minute it takes to send an SMS, or the few seconds to read a message on Twitter. By now, we have enough evidence to know that such habitual focus on the instantaneous moment diminishes cognitive memory – the capacity for recall of facts, events and people. But perhaps just as significantly, in the contraction of perception to the immediate moment, we risk losing not only the dimension of depth but of continuity – an understanding of the links between our personal past and present, of where we've been, what has formed us, how we have changed through time and where we may want to go.

Both kinds of memory are crucial to our sense of self. We are the only sentient creatures who have autobiographical memory – that is, we not only remember where we were, for example, a year ago on vacation (some animals can return to the same places on their migrations), but also the experience of ourselves being there and knowing we were the same person. Without such memory – and without a sense of continuity between our personal past and present – we would literally lose a sense of self.

On the neurological level, this is illustrated in dramatic and poignant cases of people who suffer from massive loss of memory, through Alzheimer's, for example, or brain injury. In one of his studies, 'The Lost Mariner', the neuropsychiatrist Oliver Sacks describes the case of Jimmie, who suffered from a brain injury which eliminated his ability to remember anything after his accident. Jimmy literally did not remember who he was – or who his doctor was – from one moment to another. If he left the room and returned immediately, he did not remember having been there a minute before, or recognize himself as the same person. This, of course, is a very extreme example, but it highlights the deep connections between memory and identity, and the importance of following what Richard Wollheim, in a wonderfully interesting book by that title, called 'the thread of life'.

That thread leads us not only through the external facts of our past (when we graduated, got married, divorced), but through the internalized history we carry within ourselves. In this more elusive realm, memory does not follow straight lines or chronological laws, and in order to make sense of it, we need sometimes to allow ourselves to meander through it; to let an image from the far past surface from within our minds, or to follow an unexpected leap between an event that happened, say, in our adolescence, and one closer to the present – and to muse on the meanings of such connections.

Travelling over our subjective history can also help us understand ourselves in context: to think about the background that formed us, the personalities of the people who have been important to us, the influence of our education, or how our tastes, ideas and predilections may have changed. Psychoanalysts as well as philosophers sometimes talk of 'the narrative self' – the identity we construct through putting together both our external and our internalized stories; and we need from time to time to update ourselves on that narrative – to catch up with ourselves.

The 'deep narrative' we discover within ourselves can alter considerably as our perspective, or our views, or indeed the configuration of our internal lives change. Emma, for example, revised some of her early memories of her sister, once she understood her own envious feelings towards her, and she became less suspicious towards her younger sibling – and indeed, towards others in her environment. She wasn't remembering different things, but she was remembering – and interpreting – them differently; and this gave her the sense that she had developed and grown, that her understanding of the world and of herself had deepened.

Understanding ourselves over time, rather

A diary can give you back a candid record of your outer and inner past.

than moment by moment, can help us gain a sense of inner coherence and continuity – and such continuity counts for a lot in our discontinuous lives. Memory helps ground us within ourselves, and to experience both the past and the present more intensely and richly.

Keeping a Diary

Keeping a diary belongs to a category somewhere between leisurely reflection and active mental effort. There are of course two kinds of diary. One is used to keep a simple record of the owner's appointments and activities, dinner parties and doctor's appointments. This has its uses, if only to remind us that we have been present in the past, and have done things we might otherwise have forgotten entirely. It helps us follow a sequence of events in our lives, and gives to the past a concrete reality which can be both surprising and reassuring.

But it is the other kind of diary, in which we listen to our thoughts and jot them down as they come, that is valuable as a form of deeply private reflection, and an aid to understanding the deep and long narrative of our experience. That kind

of journal probably belongs most comfortably
to the era of handwriting, and pleasing pen and
paper. The movements of the hand as it writes
apparently follow and reflect the movements of
our minds, while writing on the computer too in-
cessantly can give us carpal tunnel syndrome. But
while there is added tactile pleasure in a nicely
bound notebook and a precise pen, it is nevethe-
less possible to keep a diary on a computer as
well, if we can create a space for the kind of privacy it requires (and if we can resist looking at
those emails while we do it). Spontaneity and un-
censored observation and self-observation are of
course the key to diary-writing, and part of its enjoyment.

We don't need to spend a lot of time on keeping a journal – fifteen minutes, say, over a coffee
after work is enough if we do it consistently – but
developing the diary habit is especially valuable in
the age of the crowd-sourced, crowd-publicized
self. A private journal gives us a very different
kind of self-portrait than any number of selfies or
Facebook postings.

Marion Milner found keeping a diary ex-
tremely fruitful as she embarked on her project
of self-examination. It helped her pin down her errant and sometimes vague thoughts, and make

them real. It helped her to know what she actually felt and thought. Anne Frank, in her time of terrible trial, thought of her diary as her 'friend', and she wrote in it as if to a close intimate. Anne was an adolescent in the period when she and her family were confined and hiding in her Amsterdam attic, and the diary helped her discover new aspects of herself (including an unembarrassed eroticism, and a wicked talent for observing the foibles of others).

But for all of us, a diary can be a way of discovering as well as expressing our individual temperament, and it can give us a very particular and sometimes surprising portrait of our own personality and sensibility. 'Is this what I'm like?' we sometimes feel, as we re-read a sentence and an unexpected insight or observation comes upon us. This echoes Freud's foundational insight about the importance of articulating our experience in words – in the case of his patients, to excavate concealed memories, or to interpret disturbing sensations. But for all of us, articulation heightens clarity, and sharpens both our feelings and our perceptions. A diary is a way of conducting a most confidential and candid conversation with ourselves; and the very act of recording such conversation can give our inchoate feelings and musings a reassuring and more vivid reality.

And if we keep a diary over a long period of time, it can give us back our true personal history. We can look back at our journals and see not only what has happened in our lives, but the changes and the continuities within us: in our emotional pitch towards the world, our feelings towards specific people, and not least, our ideas or broader attitudes. Like other forms of reflection, this can also make us more cognizant of who we are, and anchor us more firmly in our experience.

5. Imaginative Exploration

To understand our experience, we need to look inwards. But our mental and imaginative resources would soon be exhausted if they were not replenished by looking outwards, and engaging imaginatively with the external world. Our minds and selves need nourishment, as much as our bodies; and if leisure has sometimes been seen as the foundation of culture, it is because it allows for the cultivation not only of self-knowledge, but of what might be called non-instrumental knowledge and non-productive aspects of the self: a disinterested curiosity, the capacity for aesthetic appreciation, the need for wonder. If we are to remain internally and intellectually alive, we need to make time not only for introspection but for imaginative exploration – for following our intellectual predilections, say, or our aesthetic impulses, without keeping an eye on the outcome or the specific goal. In a way, we need to remember that such activities are hardly superfluous; and that we need to give time to them not because they are worthy or improving, but because they enlarge our perceptions and understanding of the world, and nurture those parts of the self from which we perceive and understand.

Reading

We all know that reading is a good thing. There is no need to promote it as a fully approved activity, something that a self-respecting educated person should do as much of as possible.

But why, exactly, is it such a good thing – what do we read for? This may seem like an odd question to ask, but it needs to be posed if only because reading in the age of hyperactivity raises new questions and problems. For one thing, the very form of the book and the time required to read can seem incompatible with the digital time in which we spend so much of our lives. Our coexistence with digital devices has affected our patience and shortened the span of our attention – which often does not extend beyond the abbreviated forms of internet communication. At the same time, the problems of choice can be as daunting in our dealings with books as with other, less worthy commodities. The sheer number of books produced each year and available to us in various formats can overwhelm our ability to choose and our powers of discrimination.

Like all human activities, reading has its history and its phases, and the twentieth century was perhaps the heroic age of reading. Mastering the literary canon was part of an educated person's equipment; reading 'everything' was seen as a powerful, almost an athletic achievement. Jean-Paul Sartre, in his wonderful memoir *The Words*, describes a childhood spent almost exclusively among books – in a Parisian bourgeois household filled with these totemic objects, and dedicated to their worship. (Eventually, this period of extreme sedentary bookishness led him to develop a philosophy of action called existentialism – but that's another story.)

Mind you, young Sartre had a lot of time on his hands, as we mostly do not. Why read, then? Why should we take the time to sit down with a 'long-form' text (as it is sometimes called, in distinction to those default digital forms) and give it the requisite number of hours? There are several bad or insufficient reasons to do so, and perhaps one of the poorest is 'because we should' – because we want to be in the swim, to read what 'everyone' is reading, or as a form of high-minded consumerism, or what the writer Tim Parks calls 'this business of acquisitiveness and conquest' – so that we can tot up the number of titles we have to our credit.

Of course, we may want to read a much-discussed book for perfectly legitimate reasons – perhaps to find out why it's important, and if indeed it is; or simply to be part of the wider cultural conversation. It is after all one important role of books to stimulate such conversation, to create common points of reference within specific communities, or the wider society. Books help to create a sense that we live in a shared world, or what some sociologists have called 'imagined communities'. But the fundamental reason for taking the time to read is because books (good books, that is; books that matter) are the best aid to extended thought and imaginative reflection we have invented. In our own time, this is particularly important, as an antidote to the segmentation of thought encouraged by digital technologies. Cruising among the infinite quanta of data offered on the internet is fine for finding out information; but the disparate fragments we look at on our various screens rarely cohere into continuous thought, or a deepening of knowledge. For us, it is part of the value added

by – and the importance of – books that they require us to focus our attention and to slow down
our mental time; to follow the thread of thought
or argument until new insight or knowledge is
reached.

Unlike the flat data of the internet, books are
multidimensional; and they engage and nourish
all our mental faculties – our whole selves. There
are books that answer the basic impulse of curiosity; and for people of a certain temperament – or
perhaps for all of us, if it isn't stifled – intellectual
and imaginative curiosity can be as strong as
libidinal desire. In various studies of such things,
the urge to know has been shown to be deeply
ravelled with erotic energies, and following its
direction and urgency leads to the best kind of
reading. We may want to read a book about the latest discoveries in cosmology, or the latest studies
of ant colonies, simply because such things are
fascinating, and worth knowing; and because they
reawaken our sense of wonder about the world.
Or we may want to read a biography of a person
we admire, or a history of a period which is of
interest to us. Such books not only satisfy our desire for 'objective' knowledge, but they give us a
wider personal lens through which to view and
understand the world, and our own location within

it. They literally broaden our mental horizons and our perspective – and there is great enjoyment, as well as an intrinsic value, in that.

But it is imaginative literature – fiction, memoir, personal essays – which provides the fewest pragmatic answers to the question 'why read', and gives us the richest reasons. To make a rather sweeping proposition, imaginative literature is the art form most capable of encompassing all dimensions of human experience: the outer and the inner world, specific facts and the elusive textures of consciousness, the stories of individual selves and of the self within culture and society. Unlike factual texts which, at a pinch, can be summarized on Wikipedia, fiction and personal writing cannot be so condensed without losing something of their essence.

Reading of this kind cannot be done in a hurry. To enter a very good, or a great book (the latter are admittedly rare, but there are good reasons why we refer to them as classics), is to enter a world: the world created by the text, and the implicit world of the author's voice, style, sensibility – indeed, the author's soul and mind. This takes an initial stretching of the mind, a kind of going out of the imagination into the imaginative landscape of the book we hold in our hands. It is often a good idea to read the beginning of a book especially slowly and attentively; as in exploring a new house or place – or person – we need to make an initial effort of orientation and of empathy. Eventually, if we are drawn in, we can have the immensely pleasurable experience of full absorption – a kind of simultaneous focusing of attention and losing our self-consciousness as we enter the imaginative world of the book.

The experience of absorption in a book is both very private, and universal. A book whose reputation has lasted has been, and will be, understood by many readers across various periods and languages; it speaks to something about the human situation that apparently transcends, or over-arches, historical and cultural differences. But when we open a book we also enter a conversation between ourselves – a particular reader, with particular responses – and the text. Plunging into a novel or memoir and becoming absorbed in it calls for a certain receptivity, the willingness to 'listen' attentively to the voice of the author and the minds of others. As we follow the plot of a book, or its logical and emotional argument, it is good to pause occasionally and enter into a dialogue with the voice we're listening to – to check on what we're thinking as we read, or whether an observation or an insight strikes us as true or insufficiently so.

Our literary heritage is so enormous, and the production of new books so constant, that if one wants to give examples of what literature has to offer, one can only be very arbitrary. The writer who has been a lodestar for reflective readers for several centuries is Montaigne; his essays have been used as aids to introspection, and as stimulus to meditation on essential aspects of human experience. He was the first to coin the term 'essay' ('attempt') – to describe what he was doing – and it is a form which perfectly suits his project, which was to observe himself and others without prejudice, and to find out what he felt and thought. In a sense, he is the first modern writer to attempt the individualist route to self-knowledge – that is, a method of investigation based not on religious precepts or prior philosophical ideas, but on close and uncompromisingly honest self-observation. Perhaps that is the secret of his continual appeal, despite the fact that his style is quite old-fashioned. If his writing retains its immediacy across the centuries, that is because in his essays he gives

Delving into a book brings us into connection with other worlds and lives.

us the movements of his mind as it explores and circles around a subject, or around itself.

In a way, Montaigne was one of the first psychologists, examining himself without preconceptions and without trying to arrive at any dogmatic conclusions. He knew that the human soul (what later came to be called the psyche) is full of 'divers passions', that we are not unitary in our moods or even our deeper inclinations. He understood that pain and loss are inevitable in human lives; and he believed that insight into those emotions can make them bearable. Above all, he believed in moderation. Even virtue, he thought, 'becomes vicious, if we embrace it too stringently and with too violent a desire'. Drawing on the classical philosophers, and foreshadowing psychoanalysis, he intimated that the emotions needed to be mastered – but not stifled or repressed. But he also valued his preferences and his pleasures, which he described without prior moralism or prejudice. He wanted, above all, to preserve his quirky individuality, and the particularity of his temperament and perceptions; and this makes him excellent company, interesting and surprising on every subject. One could do worse than spend some time with him – most of his essays can be read in less than an hour – and to remember the

pleasures of self-observation, of sensing ourselves
as specific personalities with individual predilections and temperament.

Montaigne is a central monument in the literature of self-observation, but since then, the
literature of personal essay and memoir has grown
large. Before the rise of formal depth-psychology,
it was imaginative writing that gave us the richest examinations of human subjectivity. Freud
acknowledged as much when he said that poets
and writers were his true predecessors.

I still remember the sense of astonishment
when I first read Rousseau's *Confessions* – perhaps
the first work of what has been called 'deep auto-
biography'. It was written some 100 years before
the advent of psychoanalysis, but its insights extend not only to Rousseau's traits or character, but
into the origins of what might be called his neu-
roses or perversions. Amazingly, he is willing to
reveal the irregular nature of his erotic desires –
as a child, he enjoyed being beaten by a woman
who adopted him after his mother's death – and
he understands the influence of his childhood
sexuality on his adult behaviour. At the same
time, it is his capacity for pleasure – in nature, in
his own perceptions, or simply in his existence in
the world – which makes him so pleasurable to

read. 'But what did I enjoy when I was alone?' he asks. 'Myself, the whole universe, all that is, all that can be, the entire beauty of the world of sense, the whole imaginable content of the intellectual world . . .' In Rousseau's *Confessions*, the reader encounters a person exploring his inner life and giving forth his sensibility in all its contradictions. Ultimately it is the intensity with which he embraces experience, and the intensity of his quest to know himself, that underlies his sense of pleasure – and reading him puts us in touch with the more vivid registers of our feelings and thoughts.

Reading creates a sense of human fellowship. It is never (or rarely) a public activity, but in putting us in direct contact with other minds and sensibilities, it is a form of solitude which banishes loneliness. It can offer the consolation of knowing we are not alone, in our pleasures or in our suffering. It is in situations of deprivation that the value of reading – the deep need for books – becomes more vividly apparent. This was evident to me, for example, when I met ex-prisoners in Eastern Europe who had been incarcerated for their political convictions. Those who had access to books – or even remembered the contents of books they had read, and could mull them over in their empty hours – preserved their sanity and strength much better. Nelson Mandela and his fellow prisoners, labouring in the terrible conditions of an apartheid prison, administered an education to themselves through the books they were allowed to read, and memorized passages from Shakespeare. In Romania I talked to a woman who, in her time of trial, kept reading and re-reading *Anna Karenina*. This was not because it allowed her to escape into a happier or a more romantic world; quite the contrary. It was because plunging into the novel assured her that human reality was richer than the constricted world she lived in. It was because every sentence in the novel had the quality of truthfulness. It is not easy to describe that quality, except to say that Tolstoy penetrates directly to each character's inner life. His depictions of the social world his characters inhabit – their dress and domestic arrangements, the pecking order at social gatherings, their problems with work, but also, their struggles with social issues and ideological beliefs – give us a vivid sense of another time and culture; but it is his insight into the emotional texture of his characters' inner worlds – their motives and desires, their longings and painful conflicts – that gives the novel an almost three-dimensional sense of depth. Tolstoy follows not only the mercurial flow of his characters' emotions, but the logic of their consciousness – their beliefs, their changing aspirations and interpretations of their own experience.

Anna Karenina, like many great novels, shows us the lives of others in three (or actually, many more) dimensions. And this is finally why time given over to reading is time richly repaid. Literature shows us the various possibilities of being human; it increases the range of our understanding and prompts us to reflect on our own lives – to see them, perhaps, from another, or a broader perspective.

Neuroscientists, who examine consciousness by brain-imaging or analysing neurological connections, talk about certain kinds of perception or sensation called 'qualia', which so far cannot be captured through such investigations – the still ungraspable qualities of mood or emotion, the valences of pleasure and displeasure, or more delicate mixtures of thought and feeling which cannot be easily categorized. Such elusive qualities of experience are perhaps the unique domain of literature; it is not only *what* we experience, but *how*, that literature can capture better and more exactly than any other discipline or form of knowledge. Poetry and fiction give us images of human experience in all their dimensions; and great literature has the power to convince us that the complex inner lives of others are real; that others have suffered, loved and struggled as we do. Reading is not a project of moral improvement, but by broadening our perspective, it can make us less susceptible to the immediate seductions offered by our environment; and in the best-case scenarios, it can enlarge the scope of humane understanding, and of empathy.

'Art is the nearest thing to life', George Eliot said, referring to the art of fiction in particular. 'It is a mode of amplifying experience and extending our contact with our fellow-men beyond the bounds of our personal lot.'

Our contemporary forms of reading threaten to reduce that amplification. Aside from the fact that overusing digital technologies eventually makes us less mentally agile and more forgetful (as research increasingly shows), the kind of segmented, bite-sized reading we do on the internet fragments and constricts the 'space to think', instead of expanding it; in a sense, it reduces or even rubbishes our mental experience.

Our minds need to roam and stretch, to explore and discover, as our bodies do; and travelling through a long text gives us the scope for extended (perhaps on the neurological as well as imaginative level) mental exploration. But being in contact with rich imaginative worlds also reawakens and stimulates aspects of ourselves which we may forget, or suppress, if we move through our lives too fast: our capacities for reverie, lively curiosity, strenuous thought, deep insight, imagining other minds and lives.

D. H. Lawrence thought that it was better to re-read a great book six times than to read six middling books. Most of us do not have the time to revisit even a favourite masterpiece quite so often; but even if we cannot devote time to reading every evening, it is ultimately more fulfilling to spend, say, six hours a week absorbed in a complex 'long-form' text than to trawl through 600 tweets that leave little or no mark on the mind.

Aesthetic Appreciation

Of all the cultural goods available to us today, it is the visual arts which stir our most consumerist instincts. Not to acquire works of art (not many of us can afford to!), but to take tours of 'big' exhibitions, and to look at paintings or other visual artefacts. Museums in big cities are crowded to the gills; retrospectives of painters from Velazquez to Picasso draw airport-density crowds. We rush to exhibitions and rush through them, in part to have seen them – and perhaps not to miss out on something that everyone else is apparently doing.

It is hard to object to crowds flocking to museums, or the apparent increase of interest in art. It is part of being a mentally alive person to be aware of our cultural history; and it is one of the benefits of globalization that the artistic heritage of the whole world is available to us through travelling artefacts – or through our own travels. Indeed, part of the appeal of visiting museums is the seeming ease of absorbing visual knowledge. A painting can be looked at in several seconds; walking through a comprehensive exhibition of an artist's work, or of an aesthetic movement or period, takes considerably less time than reading a biography or a novel. At the same time, one of the pleasures in moving through galleries of a big museum is that images often contain a lot of information. Before the spread of literacy especially, painting was a way of conveying something about history – real or mythological – to people who could not get it from books. The Catholic church certainly understood the value of images in narrating foundational stories; and there is a whole heritage of paintings that tell us something about their period and place, or about changing mores and forms of belief, through portraits of significant figures, or depictions of various kinds of craft and labour, or scenes of marriage or battle.

This is fine, and can be a wonderfully enjoyable way of adding to our store of knowledge. But perusing paintings for their informational content, or fighting your way through an irritable crowd in order to catch a glimpse of a masterpiece, is not conducive to making contact with a rich image and what it is trying to convey to us – in other words, to a full aesthetic experience. A more than cursory appreciation of painting requires a focusing and a quieting-down of attention; a kind of mindful looking. To absorb the full meaning of a fully conceived image we need to take in not only the texture of its colours, or its lines and rhythms, but also its inwardness. We need to intuit what kind of vision – literally and figuratively – the artist has brought to the subject. Images come from deep within our psyches (we dream most often in images, after all) – and they speak to us eloquently. This is perhaps especially true of portraits and self-portraits – those representations of the human form and condition in its many aspects, from the assertions of power and shrewdness in the portraits of various Renaissance potentates, to states of dreamy reverie and trance in the depictions of (notional) saints, to visions of glamour, eroticism, despair, or modernist anxiety which have accumulated since then. Rembrandt's portraits of ageing men and women have an almost unbearable poignancy, but at the same time they remind us that ageing and vulnerability also have their human appeal, their inward beauty – if we only look at them with empathy.

Giving such attention to aesthetic objects is the very essence of a non-instrumental act. It is a useless perceptual gesture, performed entirely for its own sake. And yet, our senses and our minds need the stimulus and refreshment of aesthetic pleasure – of what used to be called beauty. In the presence of too much ugliness – which is so copiously available in our world – we grow dry and discouraged, and less able to take relish in the act of perception, and of being alive. From the Greek philosophers on, beauty has been thought to express some important principles in the universe – harmonies, or sacred symmetries – and the love of beauty was seen as close to the love of virtue or truth. ('Beauty is truth, truth beauty – that is all ye know on earth, and all ye need to know'.)

These days, we do not much talk about beauty,

and indeed, a lot of modernist and post-modern art does not in any way conform to its classical definitions or requirements. But our enjoyment of art that violates the classical rules of harmony can also be intense; and the riddle of our need for aesthetic form is being increasingly looked at through the prism of neuroscience, and sometimes, of evolution. Certain landscapes, and painterly representations of them (especially those reminiscent of the African savannah), are thought to be satisfying because they go back to the origins of our evolution, and were conducive to it; the savannah, for example, created a vantage point that protected groups from their enemies, and allowed them to evolve in peace – and later landscapes which echo such views appeal to that archaic sense of safety. In a neurological analogy to sacred symmetries, the visual arts are thought to be satisfying because they allow us to perceive certain regularities and underlying structures in what is depicted – and the perception of such regularities is important to our understanding of the world. If we cannot see patterns, we literally cannot *see* – cannot understand what is in front of us. There have also been studies which suggest that aesthetic experiences draw on 'networked' perceptual systems – that they absorb all our senses and mental powers. The best works of art give form to physical sensuality, emotion and conscious perception simultaneously, and they allow us to feel the pleasure of such integration – of feeling internally unified.

But surely our sense of beauty is also tied to a sense of attachment. The face of someone we love grows beautiful, as an unloved face doesn't. The natural and urban landscapes we grew up with remain imbricated with allure, no matter what their character. Many of my friends are baffled by my predilection for the flat, seemingly monotonous Polish landscapes, but for me, they make the strings of aesthetic response vibrate.

Of course, human and natural forms cannot be judged by the same criteria as works of art. But art reminds us that we are attached to the world through our physical perceptions – through our relish of the textures and colours of our surroundings – and it also helps us understand that the way we perceive the external world and the human form is informed by our inner vision. Hostility or fear makes the objects of our vision ugly; on the other hand, aesthetic appreciation arises out of an intense appreciation or cherishing – a way of looking that requires attentiveness and a kind of love.

Aesthetic appreciation requires keeping the doors of perception open.

Occasionally, we see faces of people in a museum looking up at a painting, rapt in focused concentration. At its most intense, the act of looking at art offers and induces a kind of total aesthetic experience. It is an act of contemplation, in what might be called the Western mode – that is, contemplation focused on an object, rather than on the emptiness within. To achieve it, we need to look with both our physical and our inner vision – to open fully the doors of perception.

Music

'All art aspires to the condition of music,' said the nineteenth-century essayist Walter Pater, and of all the arts, music most directly expresses and affects our inner states. It is also an art which happens in real time (as opposed to a book, which we can pick up and put down from day to day); and which moulds both external time and our internal pace and rhythms as we listen to it. The pace of listening to music cannot be forced (as we sometimes can quicken the pace at which we read a book); if we attempt to play an old record twice as fast, we get jarring gobbledygook. Time is the material of music, and part of its meaning; and in order to listen to a musical composition, we have to not only give it the requisite amount of real time, but to submit – give ourselves over – to its patterning of tempo and rhythm, its moulding of temporality. I'm speaking here mostly about classical music. Other kinds of music can of course be wonderfully enlivening, sexy, thrilling. But it is the works of the classical repertory which take us through extended stretches of time, and provide the experience of wordless, but often profound reflection.

Why, or how, music affects us so powerfully is, like all fundamental questions about art and mind, not easily explicable. Undoubtedly, music developed as an extension of the human voice – a faculty that proceeds from within us, and is most directly tied to emotional self-expression and our moods (try to make your voice sound really cheerful when you're feeling disappointed or dejected). Music is in part a gestural form, as the voice is; and it can give forth the movements of emotion, which always have a temporal dimension (happiness and sadness have different internal rhythms); and which, as neuroscientists increasingly observe, involve both thought and a physical, inner motion. It is not an etymological coincidence that the word 'emotion' contains within itself the word 'motion'.

It is also possible that music is directly tied to the evolutionary development of language. In a book called *The Singing Neanderthals: The Origins of Music, Language, Mind and Body*, the evolutionary biologist Steven Mithen suggests that musical communication preceded the verbal kind, rather than the other way around. Certainly, babies respond to melodious vocalizations and song long before they learn words and sentences. Indeed, babies respond to sophisticated music as well; and for parents who would keep their infants calm or give them an early injection of high culture, Mozart is the composer of choice. (Perhaps not so incidentally, having Mozart piped in to large dairies also improves the milk yield in cows. Let's face it, Mozart is good for you!)

In a way that still cannot be analysed fully, Mozart's musical language expresses states of sheer delight and deep serenity. Music rarely 'says' anything; but music speaks – and it is, above all, the language of intensity. It is hard to think of music that is merely tepid; but the language of music can encompass the most dramatic and subtle palette of feeling: tenderness, suppressed fury, madcap joy, gentle melancholy. When you listen to a Beethoven quartet, you can be taken from moods of fierce despair to robust humour, to the calmer movements of thoughtfulness and to serene, sometimes unearthly acceptance. But it is also the special trait of musical language that it can say everything at once, can suggest both grief and joy in the same chord. Chopin's harmonic progressions can compress within themselves a fierce anger and an almost erotic tenderness. It is that synthesis that music can most fully and powerfully express, and which is part of its profound effect on us.

If we want to experience the full impact and the deep pleasure of music, we need to pull away from distractions and give ourselves over to the shifts of rhythm or tonality, to the emotional modulations of a composition; and to follow its thread of development, which corresponds to a kind of thinking in sound. A friend who is a neurologist has said to me that he knows he is in a highly anxious state when he cannot become instantly absorbed in music; and he deliberately makes the effort of such immersion in order to calm down and renew his internal energies. Music, more than any other form of artistic expression, can affect and alter the listener's states: it can induce moods of great calm, or the kind of catharsis that follows a full expression of sadness or sorrow. Great compositions can move us to cry, as paintings rarely do; and often, these are tears of release and consolation. Such responses are apparently cross-cultural; and in studies that ask people to name the emotions they hear in a piece of music, the feelings identified are thoroughly consistent. We know when we're hearing joy, anger or meditative melancholy.

In his book *Musicophilia,* Oliver Sacks hazards a guess that the love of music, which is nearly universal, is akin to 'biophilia'; that we have a natural affinity for music, as we have for organic life. Music, in his poignant case studies, heals the worst symptoms of dementia; it helps post-encephalitic patients organize their movements; in cases of severe memory loss, people often remember songs and melodies after everything else is gone. It is as if music has the power to shape and bring into focus our neurological systems, to depict, through its structured motion, the patterns and dynamics of our interior lives.

It is the power of music that it enacts the drama of feeling – of 'thinking from within' – at a depth which is not easily translated into verbal language, but is nevertheless nearly universally recognizable. Music allows us to experience fully and deeply states of mind and feeling that we often keep at bay; and experiencing our inner states clearly and fully – even if they involve suffering or sadness – can be more profoundly consoling and cathartic than trying to suppress them.

We deem the idea of passion to be romantic and sentimental; but listening to music prises open those more intense and sometimes turbulent sensations and emotions which can only be called passionate. Being immersed in the musical language of Bach or Beethoven, Bartok or sometimes even Aretha Franklin, reminds us that we have inner lives which are more than superficial or politely socialized; that we have the potential for powerful feelings and responses; and that if we consign ourselves to functioning only on the surfaces of ourselves we lose rich dimensions of experience, and a measure of our humanity.

6. Contemplative Concentration

There are forms of leisure which belong somewhere between recreation and non-programmatic contemplation – or rather, which combine both. Many contemplative activities take place in natural settings, and involve a concentrated attentiveness to the natural world. Following the slow shift from light to dark as the sun sets slowly behind the horizon is a simple form of such contemplation, attuning us to a sense of the world's beauty and its poignant passing. There are also more formal kinds of natural contemplation: birdwatching is one such pastime, which requires both a training of perception and an exact knowledge of the objects observed. It also requires a patient concentration on creatures the watcher appreciates, and even loves. And it can lead (so I understand from writers' paeans, and birdwatching devotees) to a full absorption in what one is observing, and a temporary forgetfulness of oneself – or at least, of the immediate thoughts and worries that usually occupy our minds.

But among all natural activities, it is fishing – when it is done for its own sake, rather than as a way of making a living – which seems to have inspired the greatest number of devotees and of lyrical tributes. I should quickly aver that the closest contact I've had with this activity has been to watch people standing patiently on a riverbank with their extended rods plunged into the water – seemingly perfectly contented, and perfectly absorbed in the act of pure waiting; but the literature such absorption has given rise to testifies to this seemingly quietistic activity's perception-transforming powers.

The poet Ted Hughes spent many daytime and night-time hours standing still in rivers, observing their flow and the movements of life under the surface as he was trying to lure fish to his bait – and he wrote some powerfully meditative poetry capturing such moments (and his observations of nature altogether). Here, however, he describes in straightforward prose the states this patient, focused stillness can induce: 'Fishing provides that connection with the whole living world. It gives you the opportunity of being totally immersed, turning back into yourself in a good way. A form of meditation, some form of communion with levels of yourself that are deeper than the ordinary self.'

The contemplative appeal of fishing undoubtedly has to do with the watery element in which it takes place. Water is the great metaphoric element, its flow reminding us both of the ceaseless movement of time, and of nature's seemingly endless powers of renewal (although we now know that these too can be exhausted). Rivers in various cultures are mythical and holy, and watching the sea in its hypnotic ebb and flow is something that humans have surely done ever since there has been human consciousness. It is an experience which has always induced both awe and a heightened awareness of our existential situation: the impossibility of holding on to any one moment ('You can't step in the same river twice' was Heraclitus' perpetually relevant summary of this condition); our smallness in relation to nature and the cosmos, and the inevitability of death. In other words, contemplation of this primal element and force takes us temporarily beyond the limits of our individual personalities. It can induce those states in which the boundaries between ourselves and the world briefly dissolve – in which we simultaneously lose our self-consciousness and,

Contemplating the ocean puts us in touch with our finitude.

paradoxically, feel the coherence and wholeness of all our faculties. It is no wonder that experiences which involve the loss of boundaries and a sense of melding with something outside ourselves (another person, music, nature) are sometimes referred to (by Freud, among others) as 'the oceanic feeling'.

Like aesthetic appreciation, these experiences of concentrated immersion in nature are non-instrumental and unprofitable. (Of course, nature pastimes may carry the extra benefit of exercise; though if they are undertaken for the sake of toning one's muscles, then the contemplative spirit is lost.) But spending some time in proximity to nature is not only pleasurable but beneficial to our physical and mental health. It has been shown, for example, that people in big cities suffer less anxiety if they can spend some time each day in green space.

We need contact with nature for our well-being, possibly because we are attuned to the natural world and its underlying structures through the structures of our nerves and genes. We are drawn to living forms, in what has been called biophilia. If nature seems to us compelling and beautiful – if we are drawn to it with a kind of yearning – that may be because we are in some way made of the same kinds of materials. At the same time, we are not purely natural – we are human, and we live with our particular characters, inner lives and problems. If we spend too much time merging with nature (or with anything else, for that matter, like hallucinogenic drugs) we may take leave of our senses, and our individuality, for good.

But clearing a space for intervals of contemplative observation and concentration can help us still the mental noise and tensions of our daily lives, and restore a sense of perspective and distance from our immediate anxieties and preoccupations. Such moments can replenish our perceptions and our sense of wonder, and help us return to our daily lives feeling calmer and more vividly alive.

7. Choosing from Within

What is self-knowledge, and self-cultivation, for? As you consider the various forms of leisure described above, you might perhaps wonder whether what is being advocated is merely a form of self-indulgence or, worse still, navel-gazing. And indeed, it might become that – if it is carried to excess, or if it stops with treating ourselves to feasts of emotional self-awareness. But the importance of self-knowledge has always been that it helps us in choosing how to live. This is in a way the major task of any conscious life, and it has never been easy; but it is made particularly difficult by certain features of our lives and our societies, and it is worthwhile to pause and consider why that is – and how to bring the processes of self-knowledge to bear on the daily dilemmas of choice, and the long-term conduct of our lives.

If we find making choices so difficult, that is partly because we have so many of them, and because it is so easy to make them impulsively and thoughtlessly. In an interesting book called *The Challenge of Affluence*, the sociologist Avner Offer analyses the paradoxical problems caused by the abundance and novelty constantly on offer (and on show) in our prosperous Western societies. 'Affluence breeds impatience,' he writes, 'and impatience undermines well-being.' By impatience, he means the inability – or the unwillingness – to postpone immediate gratification. Why deprive ourselves of a lovely leather bag beckoning us from a shop window? Why spend the evening studying for a distant degree, when we could be going to a party? Why, in fact, resist the impulse to jump into bed with someone we met on Tinder, in the service of protecting a relationship which is just developing and uncertain?

Impatience, and the temptation to make impulsive, instantaneous choices in our daily lives, is of course greatly increased by our habituation to the rhythms of digital technologies, and the response we get from them, at a click of a mouse or a keyboard button. And following a pleasurable impulse is sometimes fine and perfectly enjoyable; but if we habitually give in to instant stimulus (of goods, or food, or sex), we may in fact achieve not gratification or pleasure, but regret – and consequences which can be quite unpleasant (frequent hangovers or unnecessary bank-debt may be among them). If we are to make good choices – and choices which are good for us – we need to distinguish what is meaningful from what is trivial, to differentiate between momentary pleasures, and our long-term aims and purposes.

On that more essential level, the process of making decisions is complicated not only by the problems of plenitude, but by an exceptional degree of individual freedom we enjoy – and struggle with – in our lives. In our contemporary, open, diverse societies, we are in principle (if not always in actual circumstances) free not only to follow our consumer preferences but, in most areas of our lives, to do pretty much what we want and as we like. We can choose the careers we want to follow, the lifestyles we want to adopt, whether to have children and in what manner to conceive them, the sex of our partners – and sometimes our own. At the same time, there have been very few societies which have offered their members so few shared codes of behaviour or assumptions about what is right or wrong, desirable or forbidden, to guide or restrict their decisions. We can choose our values, just as we choose our consumer preferences.

The temptations of plenitude and the problems

of freedom extend not only to inanimate goods, but to human beings – and to our most intimate relationships. If there are so many potential partners out there, why settle on one? And how on earth do we decide whether he or she is 'the right one'? In her book *Why Love Hurts*, a thought-provoking analysis of this problem, the sociologist Eva Illouz talks to men who leave what may seem like perfectly satisfactory relationships, out of some vague sense that somewhere out there, there may be something or someone better – someone more exciting, more compatible, or altogether less imperfect than the partners they have discarded. There are no social codes to stop them; no great opprobrium attached to serial relationships, or even infidelity; and no absolute imperative to maintain lifelong monogamy. The situation, in this respect, is somewhat different for women, who have the biological clock to contend with. But to a large extent, for women as well as for men, the easy possibility of changing partners often leads not to pleasurable hedonism, but to ambivalence and inner conflict.

Of course, there are limits our societies place on our behaviour towards others; but short of criminal transgressions, our choices, in the essential areas of life, really are individual – what we do is up to us. This is a form of personal liberty few of us would want to give up, but the lack of guiding codes for behaviour creates its own difficulties and uncertainties. It also means that the need to reflect on what we want to do, to arrive at our decisions thoughtfully, is all the greater.

To return to my rather driven friend, Peter: let's imagine that he has had an offer of a high-powered job abroad; a job which would be gratifying to his ambition, but which would be very stressful and take him away from his friends, his home, his familiar and well-loved surroundings. Peter is lucky to live in a society in which such options are open to him, but he is not without ambivalence about this offer. In the absence of all external constraints, how is he supposed to arrive at his decision? On the basis of what principles or criteria?

One method of doing so, practised by many people, is to make a list of pros and cons of the new job, and to weigh them against each other. A person favouring this method of decision-making might put, say, *better salary*, *new challenges*, *getting away from the boss*, *adventure* on the 'pro' side of the equation, and *terrible climate*, *political violence*, *leaving a promising relationship*, *uncertainty about long-term prospects* on the other.

Making decisions on the basis of such calculations is one version of what is called rational choice: that is, choice made, supposedly, in the service of our own best interests. But it turns out that ascertaining what those interests are in the first place, and following the dictates of pure reason in trying to attain them, is not at all simple. Even in the area of personal finance, where one might think the criteria for choice are simple – we want to make optimal profits from our investments – our decision-making is often driven by needs which are quite 'irrational'. There is the problem of excessive impulsiveness, in this area as in others, or of being driven by wishful thinking and unfounded hope. One instance of this was detailed in a long and poignant account by David Denby, the smart and sceptical film critic for the *New Yorker*, in which he described his obsessive quest to make a million dollars during the economic bubble of the late 1990s – in the course of which he lost a sizeable amount of money he could not afford. Denby fortunately had professional and other resources to draw on once the bubble of his fantasy had burst; but for others, the consequences of such wishful, or magical, thinking can be more destructive.

In *Thinking, Fast and Slow*, Daniel Kahneman, a psychologist who was awarded the Nobel Prize in Economics, divides human consciousness into 'System 1' – which produces our instant and involuntary perceptions, such as recognition of colours or words written in our language, and which may lead us, for example, to stop at a red traffic light without pausing to think about it – and 'System 2', which includes more complex processes of thought, and may lead us, say, to consider why traffic rules are necessary, and how they could be improved. On the basis of many precise studies, Kahneman argues that making decisions according to the subliminal system of perceptions and intuitions often works better than bringing rational considerations to them. This is partly because we are so bad at making rational predictions – at taking into account, for example, statistics on the success of investments and the causes of such success – and therefore we might as well follow our hunches as to whether we like a product or an idea on offer.

That is all very well when applied to simple, one-off choices: *I will invest in this/I will not invest in this*. Indeed, if we wanted to be coldly rational about making such decisions, we would probably entrust them to a computer and think about them no more. But what about more complex life decisions?

To follow up on Peter's not uncommon dilemma: in his case, the 'rational' process of making a list of pros and cons did not yield a convincing answer – as it wouldn't for many of us. But perhaps that is because the conception of rationality implied in the notion of rational choice is itself too limited. Arriving at complex life decisions – decisions which involve not only commodities, but our selves – cannot be done by statistical calculation, if only because we are not statistically constructed. There are companies that try to devise algorithms which calculate our conscious and unconscious consumer preferences, but this implies a horribly mechanistic idea of what and who we are. If we are not to give in to such a reduced conception of ourselves as we grapple with fundamental choices, we need to bring to bear on them a different and richer understanding of rationality – that is, an understanding which includes all our powers of consciousness, thoughtfulness and subjectivity. We need not only to compute, but to think feelingly.

This is where the fuller, more three-dimensional insights we gain through introspection and cultivation of what might be called 'deep knowledge' can come to our aid. For example, Emma, who has had some practice of self-reflection, may bring a different set of considerations to a prospect of a new job abroad. She may, by dint of understanding the sources of her hidden envy, feel less driven by the desire to over-leap one of her successful colleagues as she decides whether to accept a seemingly tempting offer. Competitiveness may become a less compelling motive, and she may be able to concentrate more fully on the personal and professional meanings the job has to her. Her father used to work for an international company, and when she was a child she thought this was very glamorous. She's still drawn to the adventure of living in an unfamiliar country, and exploring its landscapes and culture. This is a motive she doesn't disapprove of, and she may follow its call. At the same time, as she sits over a cup of coffee and ruminates, she is aware of a kind of anticipatory regret tugging at her as well – regret at the thought of leaving her nice, comfy flat, and her interesting and lively circle of friends, with whom she communicates so easily. She may not ultimately give in to this homing instinct, but she needs to acknowledge it, to stay with these more difficult or sadder feelings of potential loss for a while as she tries to arrive at her decision.

But as noted before, Emma thinks of herself as an ethical person; and as she considers the new job, she wonders whether it fits more abstract criteria of what is good or worthwhile. The reading she has done, and her sense of both the possibilities and limits of human action, may inform her thinking about this. The insights garnered from books which have been important to her have seeped into her consciousness, even if she cannot cite specific passages which have influenced her. In concrete terms, she approves of the aims of the company for which she is being recruited – a charity dedicated to improving business practices in an African country – even if she needs to find out more about the people running it. But she also feels a nagging worry, which at some point she needs to articulate, that in emphasizing her social consciousness she may be evading responsibilities and loyalties of a more personal kind: to her elderly parents, a friend who is ill and depends upon her help, a man with whom she has begun to be involved. Is her embrace of social responsibility, paradoxically, an easy way out? Is it a way of avoiding the complications of intimacy and close relationships, which she has always found difficult?

The choice Emma needs to make involves not only self-interest, but ethics; not only considerations of enjoyment, but her beliefs about what is important and meaningful, and what is not. This is a balancing act – or an act of self-knowledge – we all have to perform as we try to arrive at important decisions. We need to reckon both with our preferences – what we like and enjoy – and our values – our sense of what is good and worthwhile – and to integrate our motives with the meanings we ascribe to our actions. We do not often talk about values these days, especially moral ones; they are usually associated with conservative rhetoric, and are not generally seen as a 'cool' concept. And yet, even if we don't have a shared language of vices or virtues, we seem to be inescapably moral creatures, and our emotions and perhaps even instincts have inescapably moral implications.

The 'realist' view holds that natural emotions – those developed through evolution and for evolutionary purposes – are amoral. We need to fight our enemies for survival, and find the best breeding partners, no matter what their personality traits, in the service of those impersonal 'selfish genes'. (Hence the suspicion that the language of morality is sentimental.) But in fact, it turns out that our kinder and gentler emotions are also very much a part of our evolutionary legacy. Aside from fighting enemies, our evolutionary development has depended on the human ability to cooperate and treat each other fairly, to be attached to other members of a group, and take care of each other. Children have a passionate sense of justice, and are often upset if they or others are treated unfairly. Compassion for others, and the impulse to help if we see others in trouble, is expressed early on, and may be built into the structure of the brain. Possibly this happens via the recently discovered 'mirror neurons' – the neurons which mimic the gestures and facial expressions and moods of our interlocutors, in a kind of physiologically encoded instinct for empathy.

But in our adult lives, these nascent instincts develop into more considered attitudes and values – beliefs which direct our responses, and give our emotions particular meanings. In some cultures and circumstances, both Emma's and Peter's decisions about whether to accept or reject a new job offer might be made easier by certain shared codes of conduct. There are societies in which ambition and success are primary goods, and in which it would be a no-brainer to accept the offer of a high-powered job; there are others in which ambition is seen as faintly unsavoury, and in which attachment to your family is an overriding emotion and good. If we grew up in Japan, say, we might honour the authority of our parents or our corporation without much questioning, or be prone to a terrible sense of shame if we did not fulfil some of our responsibilities.

The dilemma facing us in our own relativist cultures is that they offer very few such norms or guidelines for what constitutes good or bad behaviour – especially in the areas of responsibility and long-term commitment. In most spheres of life, we need to mould and articulate our values through self-examination and informed thoughtfulness. We need to ponder not only what we are like, but who we want to be – what qualities or attitudes in ourselves we want to affirm, and what we do not admire. In other words, we need to create our own guideposts for important decisions – our own ethical, as well as emotional, criteria for choice.

Beyond the question of whether the new job meets her moral considerations, Emma wants to figure out how it fits in with her larger or long-term goals – the sense of purpose which she wants to animate her life. Having an overarching purpose helps us distinguish what is important from what is not, and gives orientation to our thoughts and our actions; but under contemporary conditions, finding such organizing principles for our lives is not at all easy. In a world of multiple possibilities and constant change, how do we settle on one overriding aim? How do we decide whether 'settling' on anything, or committing ourselves to plans or projects that eliminate other possibilities, is desirable – or good? Isn't it better – nobler, even – to keep ourselves open to new experiences?

In his wry and insightful memoir *A Sense of Direction*, the young American writer Gideon Lewis-Kraus tackles just this problem, and comes up with complicated answers. At a loose end in Brooklyn, he moves to Berlin, where he experiences for a while what might be called radical, hedonistic freedom. He meets other expats, most of whom refer to themselves as artists, cruises galleries with them and parties in super-cool clubs till dawn. In other words, he indulges in what should be a succession of pure pleasures; but after a while, the pleasures cease to be pleasurable at all. His lifestyle is depleting, depressing and ultimately boring. He urgently needs to find an activity that will give him a plan and an aim – what he calls, metaphorically and concretely, a sense of direction. He decides to go on a pilgrimage in Spain, and subsequently in two other countries as well.

Pilgrimages undertaken, as in his case, in a secular spirit have become very popular recently, and for good reasons. In conditions of radical freedom, a pilgrimage is a model of a certain kind of purpose. Trekking for days to a destination which once had profound religious meaning, but is now simply a clear goal at the end of a journey, gives Gideon a liberating sense of structure and a daily task which he does not need to question each morning. In a sense, it teaches him the process of making decisions – of choosing personal aims, and sticking to them. His goal is arbitrary, but it is meaningful to him; and it requires, for the time it lasts, a resolute sense of commitment. Not finishing the pilgrimage, whatever its hardships, would be a betrayal of his sense of self-esteem. (The long hours of silent walking also, not so incidentally, give him time to reflect on his emotional history quite intensely; and eventually to reconcile with his father, with whom he had good reasons to be angry.)

In our adult lives, we hope to find purposes

which last longer than the few weeks of a pilgrimage. For the classical philosophers, such basic aims were found in the quest for self-knowledge itself; or in living temperately and without excessive expectations; or in living virtuously. In our contemporary lives, such guiding principles are not available from the outside. We need to decide on our aspirations from within. But if we do so through a three-dimensional understanding of ourselves, we can endow our choices and actions with significance – that sense of meaningfulness from which true satisfaction proceeds.

We don't know what decision Emma ultimately made about her job. But she needed to give herself the space for thought in order to really know, so to speak, what she was doing, and to attain a kind of cognitive consonance about her decision – to make not only a well-calculated choice, but one to which she could give her full assent. Once she had given full brief to her motives and reasons, her uncertainty and ambivalence were replaced by a bracing sense of clarity. She knew what she wanted to do.

III. Engagement

You're on your way home from a busy day at work, feeling pleasantly tired and hoping that your partner will have started preparing a nice supper. The day passed in an odd time-zone – both very fast, and without any sense of hurry – as you concentrated on the research for an inventive new company project, had a nice chat with colleagues over lunch and went on to present your findings to a sizeable group of listeners. The project is important to you, and you spoke about it eloquently. A little while ago, all of this would have been difficult and stressful, but on this occasion, you moved through the day's paces gracefully and alertly, falling into neither lethargy nor anxiety. As you approach your home, looking forward to a pre-dinner drink, you try to identify your state, and after a while you realize what it is: you're feeling rather pleased with the day; satisfied with what you've accomplished and excited about the project's – and your own – prospects. Perhaps, you think, you're actually feeling . . . happy.

* * *

We humans are integrated systems. Our minds
and emotions, our capacity for sensuous relish
and aesthetic appreciation, our curiosity about the
world and our need for contemplative enchant-
ment, all work in concert and cannot be sepa-
rated from each other. It is only when we give
ourselves a chance to nurture all of our faculties
and ways of understanding the world that we can
begin to feel ourselves to be rich in internal resources, and to experience richly. And it is when
we allow ourselves occasionally to step away from
the constant barrage of external stimuli, and orient ourselves within our internal and external
landscapes, that we can begin to be motivated
from within – to distinguish our own desires and
preferences from the seductions of instant gratification, to discern what matters to us and what
we want to discard, to understand what we really
value and want – that is, to make choices which
are truly informed, and which we can affirm as
ours.

For this, we need time out. But most of don't
want to remain on idle permanently. We want to
use our energies, rather than let them lie fallow;
and once we have given ourselves time to renew

and deepen our perceptions and selves, we are better able to gather all of our resources and return to more active forms of experience with a full and conscious sense of engagement. I believe such engagement is what most of us desire in our lives, and in this section I will try to describe what it consists of, and some of the forms it can take in our societies today.

What is it like, what does it feel like, to be completely involved in something? Perhaps one way to put it is that it involves the ability to bring all of ourselves to an activity or an experience, without scepticism or withholding, and to focus our attention entirely on an object or a task. That requires having all of ourselves at our disposal in the first place, as well as making deliberate decisions about what we choose to do; but it also calls for a kind of self-confidence which allows us to become entirely absorbed in an activity or process of thought, without distraction or ambivalence, and sometimes to the point of 'losing ourselves' within it – or at least, losing our ordinary self-consciousness.

One interesting suggestion as to what constitutes pleasurable engagement comes from the unpronounceably named sociologist Mihaly Csikszentmihalyi and his theory of 'flow' – an idea which has been taken up by many others, in various disciplines. In his book, entitled simply *Flow*, he connects this highly enjoyable state to being entirely absorbed in certain kinds of activities, and he specifies several factors which are necessary to achieving it. The task we are performing needs to be experienced as purposeful and meaningful, so that we embark on it with full willingness; it needs to be challenging enough to keep us on the *qui vive*, so to speak, and at the edge of our abilities; but it cannot be so demanding that we feel we cannot do it, which only results in frustration. In states of flow, we often lose our sense of ordinary clock-time; a moment might expand as we home in on a detail, or several hours pass as we concentrate on solving a problem.

The activities which meet the conditions for engagement come in many varieties. Here, I will look at just a few of them.

8. Work

It is perhaps one of the big changes of the twentieth century that in our contemporary Western societies we no longer have a division between leisured and labouring classes. The great majority of us work. More than that, we largely derive our sense of value and self-worth from work. Even English aristocrats residing in their country seats (however dilapidated these may be) want to be usefully occupied. To be a modern person is to be a worker, whether you are man or woman, driven by necessity or by preference.

At the same time, our attitudes to work are often ambivalent. Centuries of experience have told us that work is a matter of necessity, something that is imposed on us; a yoke that has to be accepted, but ought to be resisted. And indeed, work is the area of life which most palpably brings us up against the limits of free choice. We can't always get what we want in the world of jobs, although hopefully we can get at least what we need.

Being part of the world of work requires us to accept the limits of our freedom and our egotism.

In the right conditions, however, work is the area of life that most clearly calls for and meets the criteria for full engagement. For most of us, work is a central source of significance and of purpose. At the day-to-day level, it affords us the energizing pleasures of delimited tasks whose goals are well defined, and, in the best-case scenario, both challenging and achievable.

How, then, can we become fully engaged in work, even in imperfect circumstances? I am not going to talk here about conditions which are unacceptable – wrongful dismissal, unjustified inequality of pay, and other social problems which the world of work, more than any other area of life, produces in every society. These are beyond the purview of this book; here, I am concerned with how we might derive from our work all the satisfaction and stimulation it can offer.

Perhaps one of the first steps is to banish what might be called excess ambivalence – a subliminal sense that, really, we're not supposed to enjoy work too much, as a matter of principle, or a kind of cultural resistance. In taking on almost any kind of job, we need to bring our full awareness to our decision: to understand what benefits of ex-

ploration or meaningful activity a particular occupation can offer us, even if it is not our ideal
choice, and what we can bring to it in return. It is
also useful to keep in mind that in our current
work structures, while we rarely have guarantees
of permanence, we don't have to think of any job
we take on as interminable. The older system of
lifelong loyalty to an institution had the advan-
tages of security, but it also had the considerable
drawbacks of stasis and stifling boredom. The
'man in the grey flannel suit' who year after year
sat at the same desk in the same office, going
through sheaves of dusty documents, hardly ex-
ists any more; for one thing, the dusty documents
have been replaced by those clean (if sometimes
too addictively compelling) computer files.

The conditions of work in our society have in
many ways improved from the days of the assem-
bly line or deadly office routine. In fact, for many
of us, the great secret is that we *like* to work. That
is what sociologists are discovering, as they study
our work habits in detail. For example, when employees of a big American company were given options to work part-time, or to take time off, many
of them did not accept the offer. This was not
mainly for financial reasons, but because many
employees – although they were reluctant to

admit it – found domestic life more stressful and more difficult than their jobs. Such findings are echoed elsewhere. They reflect the fact that time at home, especially for people with families, is fragmented among so many activities: taking children to their various engagements, dealing with accumulated emails, making supper, making sure the kids aren't watching pornography online, etc. This can create stressful pressures and scattering of attention, and exhausting demands to keep making small and bigger choices. A friend who has growing children and a large circle of friends remarked that work is the most restful thing she can do; finally, she can be in one place at one time, and bring her mind to a concentrated task.

Purposeful concentration is one of the conditions of flow, but in order to achieve it we need to give our assent to the job we are doing, even if we are conscious of its limitations. It helps, also, to know ourselves well enough that we do not over-estimate – or underestimate – our abilities.

But if we plunge into a job willingly, and give ourselves over to its demands (without succumbing to those ever-present digital distractions), then we can derive great satisfaction from the structured effort that most work involves: from performing a task to its completion, without the nagging sense that we might be – or maybe should be – doing a dozen other things. Whether we are trying to make something or to solve more abstract problems, work presents us with tasks which are by definition useful, and whose aims are delimited and defined. It allows us the luxury of focused attention as we grapple with a problem or process. In that sense, work is an antidote to mental dispersion and fragmentation; and in presenting us with new challenges, many jobs can stretch us to exercise our mental capacities strenuously, and discover in ourselves innovative ways of thinking, or abilities we didn't quite know we had.

A sense of competence and accomplishment, as well as the adventurousness of tackling new problems, is one of the energizing pleasures that work can offer us. The other is collaboration. Most of us still work in institutions rather than at home, and most jobs require at least occasional collaboration with colleagues, and collective decisions. (Even if we work from home, our activities are addressed to others, and often need their input and contributions.) But there are also forms of endeavour in which collaboration is an intrinsic part of the work process. As anyone who has worked at an architectural office, say, or a newspaper knows,

putting together a complicated product or project – one which calls for disparate skills and
parts – requires a constant and precise level of
cooperation. In order for a newspaper (an institution where my main experience of collaborative
work comes from) to appear each day, the writer
has to deliver the piece, the editor to make sure
the piece meets certain standards, the printer to
put through each page in time, and hopefully
without too many errors. In order for this to happen, each person involved has to contribute their
part on time and without demanding special attention or considerations – at least while the task
is being completed. Tempers occasionally flare
up, and disagreements break out; but everyone
understands that these cannot go on for long –
that the job has to get done, and for the moment,
personal concerns have to be put aside.

The pleasure we take in such collaboration
can be great. It is the enjoyment of solidarity – of
working with others towards a particular goal, and
achieving something we all value. The relationships involved are not necessarily personal; indeed,
they require us to put aside, for the duration of
the task, the preferences we may feel for particular colleagues, or our antagonisms. But the solidarity we feel with others is in itself what might

be called an impersonal emotion – a sense of invigorating satisfaction that comes from participating with others in a collective effort, and from knowing that we can count on each other to contribute our part. This implies a kind of impersonal trust in others, as well as in ourselves. We cannot collaborate effectively if we are feeling excessively insecure, or superior to our colleagues.

Even in less collaborative jobs, if we work in the spirit of pure competition, or if we are perennially resentful because we feel we are underestimated, that may prevent us from being absorbed in the content of what we are doing – and therefore, from enjoying our jobs and doing them well. The instinct for cooperation runs deep, and is built into our evolutionary history. Certainly, animal groups have to achieve a certain degree of cooperation in order to survive; and we humans could not have built our cultures and civilizations through solitary endeavour. At the same time, in our highly competitive and stress-inducing societies, the collaborative impulse is easily undermined. In order to reclaim its pleasures we also need sometimes to step back from the fray, and reckon with internal attitudes. Work requires not only specific skills but emotional self-awareness;

and time spent in self-reflection is well repaid in work satisfaction, and perhaps even success.

Admittedly, I have been talking mostly about middle-class jobs. It is undoubtedly much harder to achieve satisfaction if you work in a factory which produces, say, computer chips in an assembly-line process. Even in such places, though, physical environments are no longer as infernal as they once were, and employees may experience the enjoyment of a task well done as well as the pleasures of sociability and solidarity. In *Flow*, Csikszentmihalyi describes Joe, who worked all his life as a welder in a Chicago plant where railroad cars were assembled. Joe enjoyed mastering various aspects of the plant's operations so much that he refused to become foreman, a promotion that would have deprived him of physical involvement in his work.

It is possible that states of flow are easier to attain in work that draws on physical skills as well as mental ones, and therefore helps us achieve a kind of mind–body integration. Indeed, it should be no surprise to find that many varieties of work not classified as 'white-collar' can be a source of pleasure and satisfaction. Farming can surely be seen as a 'holistic' activity (just think of *The Archers*), no matter what its physical or, sometimes, economic hardships. Certainly, traditional farmers in parts of the world which have not been subject to full modernization often express a deep attachment to their way of life. In more modernized circumstances, devising or construct- ing better machine parts, say, can be a high form of craft. Such jobs should, and probably will, become more respected as our physical skills threaten to decline – not least because of our ever-increasing reliance on the internet – and as we begin to admire them, sometimes with nos- talgia.

Work, above all activities, engages what are sometimes called 'social emotions' – our need for respect and recognition, but also for cooperation and extending respect to others. Such needs are central to our sense of self, and apparently pro- ceed from regions of our brains involved in the most fundamental emotions. The neurological signals of admiration are as powerful as those in- volved in the feelings of love. Whatever society we live in, we want to be esteemed by our colleagues and fellow workers – indeed, by our fellow humans. But in order to be able to experience esteem – to recognize the recognition, so to speak – and in order to extend it to others, we need to achieve a kind of internal balance in which we are neither too insecure nor too egotistical to see others as our colleagues and equals.

Purposeful activity and collaboration are the invigorating pleasures of work; but perhaps the main good and psychic benefit we derive from it – so obvious as to go too easily unnoticed – is a sense of usefulness. The need to feel useful runs deep in us, and is closely aligned with our need for a sense of purpose. We are social animals, and in order to feel that we matter, we need to be needed as well as esteemed or loved. To be affirmed as part of any group or community, we want to feel valued for our contribution to it. Of course, we baulk at being considered *merely* useful or instrumental, but work is an area of life in which we can temporarily subsume our particular personalities in the service of the impersonal needs of a group or a common aim – and (perhaps by a dynamic analogy with contemplative concentration) feel ourselves to be not diminished but enlarged thereby.

9. Relationships

'Work and love' was Freud's formulation for what was important in life, the central aspects of experience from which we derive meaning and pleasure. We don't much talk about love nowadays, but relationships continue to be of primary significance to all of us. At the same time, no area of experience has been affected more dramatically by digital technology than relationships in all their guises – from friendship to sociability to collegiality and, indeed, intimacy and love.

On the one hand, digital technologies widen the reach of our acquaintance and our access to others incrementally; most of us 'know' hundreds more people than we ever did before, and across a larger geographic territory. But what is meant by 'knowing' others has changed enormously. We 'talk' with each other voicelessly, via texting or Facebook; and we communicate with each other en masse, in Twitter-sized sound bites. Even sexual relations – formerly a privileged realm of deep privacy and complex passions – are increasingly conducted via dating apps such as Tinder, on the basis of snapshot information and with no necessary assumption of emotional involvement.

Perhaps, occasionally, such virtually arranged encounters can result in a *coup de foudre* – an instant attraction that turns into intimacy and leads to a long-term relationship. But mostly they don't, and like other forms of hedonic behaviour, they all too often lead not to pleasure or mutual knowledge but to a stale sense of disappointment and deprivation.

Authentic human contact is the basic foodstuff of the psyche; in its absence, we become internally arid and diminished. There is a danger, however, that in our increasing reliance on digital communications we may be losing track of what such contact is, or how we can achieve it. In an important book, *Reclaiming Conversation*, Sherry Turkle, a clinical psychologist who has written intensively about the effects of digital technologies on our inner lives, worries that in losing our habit of face-to-face conversation we are also losing the all-important capacity for empathy – for understanding other people's minds and feelings. In studies of today's elementary school pupils, it appears that in marked contrast to previous generations, such

Plato Conversing with his Pupils – dialogue is foundational to philosophy, and to humane understanding.

children prefer their iPads and mobile phones to talking or playing with others; and that therefore their capacity for empathy, which usually develops quite naturally – the ability to recognize what other children feel, and act accordingly – is severely reduced. Digital children can be unwittingly mean to their schoolmates without realizing they are being hurtful, or reading the signs of other children's distress. Moreover, in our adult lives, we also increasingly prefer digital messaging to face-to-face contact. Our pleasure centres light up when our mobile phones signal a message, and we routinely allow virtual communications to interrupt our *in vivo* exchanges. The curtailment of basic human skills early on, and the loss of human contact in our adult lives, has worrying implications for all of our social and personal relationships – for the development of generosity and compassion, and for our ability to judge others' motives accurately.

Conversation – of the embodied, face-to-face kind – is of course the basic currency of human exchange, and is a way not only of knowing others, but of understanding ourselves. Indeed, we could hardly become ourselves, or know anything much, in isolation. Our identities initially develop through our early relationships with others, and our later understanding expands through various kinds of dialogue: with books, with teachers, peers and friends. Socrates conducted his philosophical teachings through dialogue; and dialogue is at the heart of depth-therapy and psychoanalysis (which in its first days was, after all, called 'the talking cure').

It's good to talk, and in some cultures and periods conversation was considered a high art, with settings dedicated to its cultivation. The French salon – that supposedly dandyish and frivolous institution – often had a serious purpose: to bring together like-minded people in order to discuss issues of the day outside the hierarchy and the ritualized forms of the royal court. In all registers – from sociability to collegiality, from teaching to political debate and informal discussion – conversation is a way of thinking with others; of testing our own and others' ideas, in a free and playful flow of shared thought.

But this happy combination of spontaneity and absorption requires, above all, unscripted time. In a piece called 'The Myth of Quality Time', Frank Bruni, a *New York Times* columnist, describes a family ritual in which twenty members of an extended family gather at a beach house for a 'solid week' – an amount of time which his friends find shockingly long, but which most people even a few decades ago would have found positively mingy. Bruni contrasts this form of being together with the notion of 'quality time', in which we dutifully set aside a pre-planned hour or two for what is, in effect, another task – girding yourself to pay close attention to another person. Bruni's unscripted week, in contrast, allows for the unexpected observation and the spontaneous encounter to emerge. 'With a more expansive stretch,' he writes,

> there's a better chance that I'll be around for the precise, random moment when one of my nephews drops his guard and solicits my advice about something private . . . Or when one of my siblings will flash back on an incident from our childhood that makes us laugh uncontrollably . . . There's simply no real substitute for physical presence.

This should be obvious, but is becoming less so. In a way, we need to relearn what, for most people throughout much of history, came rather naturally: the habit of being with others, and learning about them through physical proximity as well as conversation and disclosure. Attraction can be instant, but forming a bond with another person – whether it is in friendship or intimacy – requires a particular kind of attentiveness, and the kind of time in which we can follow the train of another person's thought, or absorb their mood or expressive gaze without driving to a conclusion or thinking impatiently about our next appointment. The French philosopher Emmanuel Levinas thought that the source of all meaning and significance resided in the individual human face. In coming to know another person, we need to learn how to 'read' their expressive language as well as their verbal utterances.

Indeed, the ability to be with others and to understand them is not very different from the ability to be with ourselves, and to know ourselves from within. We can only recognize emotions and responses in other people if we have experienced and understood them ourselves. In order to enter another person's inner landscape, we need to have travelled our own, and to have opened various areas of thought and feeling. If these are closed off within ourselves, then we do not have the instruments of perception with which to understand another person.

This does not mean that we need to abolish all distance, or separateness, between ourselves and others, or to merge with them to the detriment of losing our own agency or identity. In a way, the need for boundaries also mimics our relationship to ourselves, and the need for some detachment from our own impulses or emotions. The process of arriving at self-knowledge involves some separation from our unexamined impulses, or aspects of ourselves which we do not value. And, if our relationship to another person is to be one of equals, we also need the combination of empathy and boundaries. Empathy is not the same thing as automatic sympathy; if we find ourselves in conflict with a close friend or intimate, it is a better part of respect to say what we really think, rather than pretend anodyne agreement. If a partner engages in some small act of dishonesty or betrayal, a failure to express our disappointment or even anger may only suggest indifference or a lack of trust. For that matter, if a person we care about is struggling with some internal problem – say, they feel perennially underestimated by their colleagues – it is not sufficient to say 'There, there, of course you're right – you are great and they are fools.' That might be as unhelpful as it is unrealistic. Again, it is a better part of mutual respect to examine with the other person where the problem may actually lie – just as we might want to examine such a difficulty within ourselves. For this, we might want to delve more deeply into the causes of the problem with them, and find out together whether, for example, they are afraid to do their best for fear of failure; or whether they might be overestimating themselves, and therefore taking offence at others' appraisal of them.

That level of honesty calls for a great deal of trust. It requires us to apply the same standards of concern, love and realistic judgement to our friends and intimates as we apply to ourselves. Doing unto others as we would have them do unto us, if it is understood deeply enough, turns out to be a demanding motto and imperative. It requires not only a principled respect (necessary though that is to our social relations) but, at the intimate level, a recognition of another person as a full human being with emotions and a mind like our own.

Of course, giving extended time to any one person is complicated by the same problems of proliferating choice that riddle our decisions in other areas of life. Dating sites increase the sense that there is countless plenitude of available partners. Why stop our search, or decide prematurely that one (always imperfect) potential partner will do? In a way, this is a version of a syndrome that

Intimacy begins with entering the language of another person's face.

has become prevalent enough to acquire an acronym: FOMO, or fear of missing out. Just what are we missing out on? What exciting things could we be doing, what fantastic people could we be meeting, at any one moment – or at least, on any one extended evening? FOMO used to be a phenomenon limited mostly to adolescents who dreaded not being invited to the right parties, but it now extends itself at least to young adults, and often further.

The seemingly endless availability of potential partners, combined with the almost complete lack of restrictions on sexual behaviour, mitigate against commitment; but as a gathering body of studies and personal testimony shows, this does not lead to greater satisfaction – any more than hedonic dispersion and impulsiveness lead to well-being in other areas of experience. In this all-important dimension of our lives, we also need to make our choices not in response to external stimuli, but from within. We may no longer believe in the romantic idea of 'one and only' object of love, but close relationships conducted with trust and candour remain the most fulfilling form of engagement and the most authentic source of meaning we know. Coming to truly know another person – whether it is a romantic partner or a friend – calls for all our powers of thought and the full palette of emotional perception. At the same time, such relationships allow us to express our individuality – our particular preferences, foibles and quirks – more completely than we can in any other area of experience; and therefore to be known and appreciated in three dimensions.

In contrast to virtual knowledge, which takes place in the flat spaces of computer screens and via abbreviated communications, intimacy proceeds from inter-subjectivity – an interplay of subjectivities which calls for authenticity of response, and a kind of reciprocal depth perception. In bringing all of ourselves into play, and in being perceived three-dimensionally, we come to experience our personalities and inner lives more vividly and richly – to exercise our full human intelligence. Our subjective selves need to be touched, as our bodies do. If we ever feel guilty or restless about giving open-ended time to an intimate or a friend, we need to remember that being with others – knowing others and being known in depth – is essential to our happiness, as well as to living a fully humane life.

10. Creative Play

Work and relationships are the central pillars of our lives – at least, as most of us wish to live them; but there is another kind of activity which can engage us completely, and which both philosophers and psychoanalysts have considered just as essential to our development, and, indeed, to the development of culture. This is the often underestimated category of creative play. Although 'play' in all its forms can be highly pleasurable and involving, I would like to distinguish creative play from such activities as games or sports, in which the rules are prescribed in advance and the aim – winning – strictly and narrowly defined. By creative play, I mean something both more improvised and more – well, creative; that is, activities which leave room for imaginative exploration and discovery, as well as for unexpected results. Of course, play pervades many areas of life. Both work and relationships contain elements of happy playfulness, if we have achieved a certain level of ease and spontaneity within them; scientific discoveries are not infrequently made by dint of playful experimentation; and creative endeavour almost necessarily involves elements of playing around – with sounds, paint or words – as well as intense mental and imaginative effort.

In a wonderful book called *Homo Ludens: A Study of the Play-Element in Culture*, Johan Huizinga, a Dutch philosopher, suggests that both art and ritual, as well as (on the less happy end of the spectrum) war, emerge from a kind of playfulness: giving form which is both gratuitous and serious to important human activities, and to early intuitions about the human relationship to the universe or to each other. In Huizinga's analysis, our very ability to know emerges from a kind of conceptual playfulness. He particularly mentions certain archaic games – riddles, formal exchanges of questions and answers – which may be a very early form of gaining understanding through dialogue, of a back-and-forth between an acolyte and a spiritual authority. (Sometimes, such early games were played for pretty high stakes: if you couldn't answer the 'fatal riddle' of the Sphinx, death awaited!)

If play is at the root of culture, it is perhaps because the ability and the need to play seem to be built not only into our nature, but the nature of much animal life. Cats and dogs certainly play not only with each other, but with humans, as anyone who has had pets can testify. In children, the ability to play arises naturally if it is not hampered, and is necessary to full development. In the observations of the British psychoanalyst W. D. Winnicott, the child initially plays in the 'safe space' created by the proximity of a caring adult, by experimenting, say, with various arrangements of blocks. Such experimentation seems to be both an urge and a need of human consciousness; and in Winnicott's view, it is the origin of later cultural activity and the serious play of creative work.

We don't have to be classified as 'creative workers', however, to feel the appetite for creative play or to benefit from its pleasures. There are cultures which have rich traditions of amateur creativity and experimentation, and British history is filled with examples. (Darwin, after all, was an amateur, and pursued his preoccupations without any assurance of results or rewards.) Before the beginning of the digital era, London (and undoubtedly other parts of the British Isles) was home to a wide variety of amateur activity in its still less hectic precincts: amateur chamber music groups and theatrical performances; people trying to breed new varieties of plants, or create devices for body-propelled flight. Possibly some very concrete results came out of such experiments, although for the people involved that was not the main point. 'Amateur' means literally 'lover of', and amateur endeavours are undertaken for the love of the thing itself. For the people engaged in them, such activities constitute a kind of 'free space' in which to give vent to their curiosities and abilities, without the constraints of competitiveness or worry.

At the same time, in order to be enjoyable, creative activities have to be undertaken seriously enough to be executed at a certain level of competence. Performing a Haydn quartet is no fun if it consists mostly of halting phrases and wrong notes; the point of staging an Oscar Wilde comedy, however informally, is lost if the actors muddle up their entrances and lines. Work contains elements of play, and in order to be pleasurable, creative play has to contain an element of strenuous effort – of concentration and discipline. It also needs to have form and structure. Both in childhood and later on, play is the non-instrumental use of the imagination, allowing it to wander where it will – but it turns out that the imagination, if it is allowed free rein, looks for and finds structure pretty fast. Children improvise rules for

The urge to play is instinctive in children, and intrinsic to much cultural activity.

their interactive games – otherwise, they are not games, and no fun. Mature creativity also needs to find its forms in order to be satisfying. Playfulness gives expression to the sheer vitality of consciousness, and it depends on improvisation and cognitive flexibility, but it may also be a demonstration of our need to make sense of what we perceive and discover.

In the digital era, amateur activities have largely been replaced by virtual games, which are both a huge business and, for their devotees, a diverting and sometimes highly addictive pastime. It may be that such games increase alertness, as some of their advocates claim. But they do not call on our capacities for inventiveness or mental exploration. The invention, in these games, has already been done for you; the player's role is to respond, even if the range of response can be fairly wide. Crucially, digital games do not engage our bodies or physical skills. They involve the same limited actions as all our other transactions with digital technologies: the clicking of buttons, or moving a computer mouse on a desk surface.

In contrast to the constricted spaces of digital games, creative play is a way of exploring and expressing the full range of mental and imaginative possibilities freely, and most often through physical action. This can be as meaningful and absorbing as more functional or ostensibly serious projects. One famous example of someone who took creative exploration very seriously, even while being involved in the most serious possible endeavour, was Winston Churchill, who throughout much of his career remained a dedicated amateur painter – and for whom this 'pastime' played an important role in his emotional life. Churchill, who suffered from lifelong depression (which he called his 'black dog'), said that painting 'came to his rescue' at a difficult time, and he devoted many hours to it throughout his career, even as he was commanding armies during World War II. This, for him, was hardly a frivolous hobby. Indeed, he compared thinking about painting to the process of making strategic decisions; and it may be that allowing our minds to move freely, whether in considering a scientific problem or the form of a painting, is the best way of arriving at complex conclusions and decisions. Churchill did not have professional ambitions as an artist, but he worked hard at it and gave it his entire concentration; and his reward was what we would now call the state of flow. 'I know of nothing which more entirely absorbs the mind,' he wrote. 'All one's mental light becomes concentrated on the task.'

Play may seem like a cultural luxury, an extra; but cultures that lose their ability to play become repressive and static (think of the more severe forms of sharia law, with their restrictions on aesthetic pleasure). Indeed, in its various forms – from high to low, from frivolous to serious – play may be both at the root of culture, and one of its high achievements: an expression of basic human freedom, and of the need for freedom in order to be fully ourselves.

Conclusion

There are many ways to live; but to live meaning-lessly is to miss your life. If we rush through our days and months in ceaseless activity, and without taking stock of what we're doing, we can soon lose track of what we are doing it for, or why it matters to us. If we are not to move through our activities mindlessly, or to denude our experiences of significance and depth, we need to orient our-selves in our lives – and within ourselves: to muse, relish, reflect and occasionally even to be bored.

In order to live lives worth living – so the old philosophers taught us – we need to know who we are, and to be guided by deliberately chosen aims and purposes; and for that, we need, in our busy lives, to give time to the cultivation of knowledge, and the practices of self-knowledge. We live in de-manding, individualistic, diverse societies – and beyond that, in a complex, interconnected, often turbulent world. The conflicts, catastrophes, tri-umphs and ordinary human struggles in all parts of the globe enter our lives via vivid images on television screens or on those smaller ones. Such awareness implicates us; and it is part of being a sentient and responsible person to think about the larger world we live in, and respond to it in ways which reflect our values and our understanding. But if we are to give value to our own lives, we also need to nurture our perceptions and internal resources, to cultivate our capacity for play and pleasure, and to draw on our knowledge and self-knowledge in order to use ourselves wisely and well. A sense of meaning which allows us to be fully alive comes from our involvement with others and engagement in the world; and it comes, above all, from within.

Homework

I. The Problem

Digital addiction is an omnipresent contemporary problem, and the literature about its effects on our selves and brains is large and growing. I have found several books about it informative and useful:

The Shallows: How the Internet Is Changing the Way We Think, Read and Remember by Nicholas Carr is an impassioned disquisition on the profound (and in his view mostly negative) impact of the internet on our minds and brains – our capacity to think, read and store experiences in long-term memory. Carr is a writer about technology, and this is no Luddite tract; but his arguments are personally felt and comprehensive.

Mind Change: How Digital Technologies are Leaving Their Mark on Our Brains by the neuroscientist Susan Greenfield also tackles the effects of pervasive technological change on our brains, identities and relationships. It's very accessible, and leavened with some personal examples and anecdotes.

Richard Restak's *The New Brain: How the Modern Age is Rewiring Your Mind* is another neurologist's take on digital overuse and the speeding up of our lives, and is particularly good on the effects of multitasking and the impact of digital technologies on young brains – and therefore, on the next generation's. It is accessible and clear.

Renata Salecl's *The Tyranny of Choice* is a short, reader-friendly book on the anxieties induced by the illusion of free choice, and by the idea that we can change our identities and lives for the better by following a few tips on how to do so. The ideology of choice, Salecl argues, is at the centre of the consumerist society, and it breeds the idea that we can shop for ourselves as well – and diverts us from struggling with more serious social issues. Salecl's argument is somewhat ideologically loaded, but worth listening to.

Why Love Hurts by Eva Illouz is an original and incisive study of how the wide-ranging availability of potential partners, and of sexual choice, has lessened the incentive to commitment among men. Illouz is particularly good on the historical shifts in relations between men and women, and the changes wrought by the sexual revolution.

II. Leisure

Leisure: The Basis of Culture by Josef Pieper is an eccentric but fascinating book written by a religiously inclined philosopher, wherein he argues that leisure is the foundation of Western culture, and of its philosophic tradition – and that modernity has supplanted this ideal with the tyranny not so much of work itself, as the ideology of work. Even thinking, Pieper argues, has become reformulated as 'intellectual work', rather than being understood as the capacity for contemplation and wonder – for the authentic 'philosophic act'. 'Leisure' is so outside the mainstream of our current thinking as to be thought-provoking.

'In Praise of Idleness' by Bertrand Russell is a diverting, rather dandyish essay, arguing that we have overdone the ethos of work, and that we would be much better off working only four hours a day.

For the processes of introspection, there is a large body of psychoanalytic classics, to stimulate thinking about the patterns of internal life. Freud is a wonderful writer, and his case studies read like intriguing detective fictions, pursuing clues contained in symptoms and dreams, to get at deeper psychic truths.

A Life of One's Own by Marion Milner (aka Joanna Field) is a beguiling account of one person's attempt to understand herself, and to disentangle her own desires, preferences and sources of pleasure from the cultural pressures and imperatives which have formed her. In *An Experiment in Leisure*, she continues to examine herself with the aid of images which have been important to her – from mythology, religion, art and her own memory. A wonderful companion to one's own experiments in self-knowledge.

Adam Phillips's many books and essays are stylish, often whimsical, and informed by literature and philosophy as much as by psychoanalysis. *Darwin's Worms* is an extended meditation on the need to accept mortality as part of our human condition, and in order to value more intensely the time we actually have in our lives. *Going Sane* is valuable for affirming the temperate state of sanity and the pleasures of normalcy, against assumptions about the 'creative' value of neurosis and extreme mental states.

For a more scientific approach to the mind's

ways, Antonio Damasio's *Self Comes to Mind* is a fluently written and rigorously argued investigation of the complex interactions between feelings and meanings, emotions and the brain, in the construction of consciousness and sense of self. Damasio is a neuroscientist who is interested in the human psyche, and his account of how our perceptions and selves are constructed makes for stimulating reading.

Gerald Edelman's *Wider Than the Sky* is a meticulous analysis of the neurological processes which go into the basic act of being conscious – with some mysteries still unsolved.

In a fictional vein, Virginia Woolf's *To the Lighthouse* captures lyrically and precisely the movements of her characters' minds, in states of reverie, free-association, and moments of contemplative epiphany.

Proust's *Remembrance of Things Past* is of course one of the greatest and most beautiful literary meditations on the strata of memory, and the presence of the past within us. Its several volumes can be savoured over several holidays, or as a reading pleasure for a year.

There are countless books on the pleasures and merits of reading, music and art. This is a very arbitrary selection of texts which bring to these age-old themes some contemporary concerns.

Alberto Manguel's *A History of Reading* is a compendious and enjoyably digressive history of this activity, showing how the manners and morals of reading have changed over the centuries (it took a while for people to learn how to read silently!), and why the act of reading is so important to the development of literature, the life of cultures and the cultured life.

Stop What You're Doing and Read This! is a collection of ten essays by contemporary writers on the importance of reading actual books. Passionate, personal and varied in their approach, the essays remind us why reading matters, why it is so enriching, and why it is an essential form of connection to others, and to the world.

The Aesthetic Brain: How We Evolved to Desire Beauty and Enjoy Art by Anjan Chatterjee is a neuroscientist's up-to-date take on the aesthetic impulse. Chatterjee clearly appreciates and enjoys art, and his theory of 'neuroaesthetics' combines the idea of integrated perception with the proposition that our responses to art are ravelled with other forms of pleasure – in food, sex, and even money.

Musicophilia by Oliver Sacks is an examination of musical cognition, why and how music is so deeply embedded in the brain and memory, and why it has such powerful effects on us, for good and sometimes ill. Sacks was a neurologist with a flair for the quirky case study, and here, he gives some diverting examples of both the disturbances of the musical sense, and instances of surprising musical ability. He is particularly moving on the power of music to heal, and to sustain a sense of self in the face of its loss.

The Singing Neanderthals by Steven Mithen is a fascinating book, drawing together evidence from archaeology to child psychology, and the study of birdsong and primate communication systems, to posit the hypothesis that music precedes spoken language and leads to its development.

On the process of making choices and decisions, I particularly like Avner Offer's *The Challenge of Affluence* – a thought-provoking sociological study of how an excess of choices in various areas of life affects our ability to make decisions, control our impulses, or commit ourselves to long-term goals. Rife with statistics and case studies, this is nevertheless a readable book about the challenges to well-being paradoxically posed by affluence – and it is suggestive about the need for some self-control and long-term thinking.

III. Engagement

On the pleasures of engagement, Mihaly Csikszentmihalyi's books on 'flow' (*Beyond Boredom and Anxiety: Experiencing Flow in Work and Play; Flow: The Psychology of Optimal Experience*; and others) offer perhaps the most promising propositions on how to achieve states of full involvement and absorbed satisfaction in work and play.

In *Together: The Pleasures, Rituals and Politics of Cooperation*, Richard Sennett, a philosophically informed sociologist, talks about the urgent need, in our diverse societies, to learn the practices of cooperation and solidarity, on every level from work to civil society – and to be engaged with others in collaborative rather than competitive ways.

In *Reclaiming Conversation: The Power of Talk in a Digital Age*, Sherry Turkle reminds us that conversation is crucial to all forms of relationship and knowledge, and that in shifting to digital communications in lieu of living contact, we are in danger of degrading our capacities for empathy, learning through dialogue and for forms of public debate. We need to reclaim the space for conversation in order to nurture forms of contact basic to our common culture and our humanity.

For a historical attempt to capture good talk before the digital age, read *The Age of Conversation* by Benedetta Craveri – an un-nostalgic history of the French salon in the seventeenth and eighteenth centuries, and the rise of conversation as a highly valued skill. Full of diverting facts about who was there, and who said what to whom, *The Age of Conversation* is also a serious look at the salon as an important political institution and space for unofficial discussion.

For the value of play, *Homo Ludens* by Johan Huizinga is the classic, but probably still unsurpassed text. Huizinga, a Dutch historian who was one of the founders of cultural history, looks at the origins of culture in the 'play element' of ritual, spectacle, riddles and games. An original and fascinating book, giving us glimpses of sensibilities very different from our own; and at the same time, reminding us that play is a basic feature of many human activities, and the basis of the creative imagination.

Children's Games in Street and Playground by Iona and Peter Opie is a study, based on extended observation, of games – sometimes very rough – generated and invented by children themselves. The Opies were students of children's 'folklore', and offer wonderful evidence of children's need for play, and their spontaneous creativity, when they are left to their own devices. A book about play in the pre-digital age.

Photographic Credits and Permissions Acknowledgements

Page 102 Palm Tree and Person on Beach by Kevin Tyler © Special Photographers Archive / Bridgeman Images

Page 139 *Plato Conversing with his Pupils*, from the House of T. Siminius, Pompeii (mosaic) / Museo Archeologico Nazionale, Naples, Italy / Bridgeman Images

Page 146 Couple toasting with wine in cafe © Blend Images via Superstock

Page 153 Children Playing 'Twinkle, Twinkle, Little Star', Flint Street School, Southwark, London, 1908 © City of London: London Metropolitan Archives / Heritage Images / Getty Images

The quotes from *A Life of One's Own* by Marion Milner on pages 44–45 and 56 are reproduced by kind permission of Routledge.

The quote from *Self Comes to Mind* by Antonio Damasio on pages 59–60 is reproduced by kind permission of Vintage.

Explore All of the "Maintenance Manuals for
the Mind" from the School of Life Library

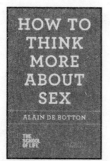

How to Think More About Sex
Alain de Botton
ISBN 978-1-250-03065-8 / E-ISBN 978-1-250-03066-5
www.picadorusa.com/
howtothinkmoreaboutsex

How to Stay Sane
Philippa Perry
ISBN 978-1-250-03063-4 / E-ISBN 978-1-250-03064-1
www.picadorusa.com/
howtostaysane

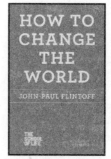

How to Find Fulfilling Work
Roman Krznaric
ISBN 978-1-250-03069-6 / E-ISBN 978-1-250-03070-2
www.picadorusa.com/
howtofindfulfillingwork

How to Change the World
John-Paul Flintoff
ISBN 978-1-250-03067-2 / E-ISBN 978-1-250-03068-9
www.picadorusa.com/
howtochangetheworld

PICADOR

www.picadorusa.com

Available wherever books and e-books are sold.

Explore All of the "Maintenance Manuals for
the Mind" from the School of Life Library

How to Be Alone
Sara Maitland
ISBN 978-1-250-05902-4 / E-ISBN 978-1-250-05903-1
www.picadorusa.com/
howtobealone-maitland

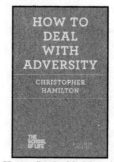

How to Deal with Adversity
Christopher Hamilton
ISBN 978-1-250-05900-0 / E-ISBN 978-1-250-05901-7
www.picadorusa.com/
howtodealwithadversity

How to Think About Exercise
Damon Young
ISBN 978-1-250-05904-8 / E-ISBN 978-1-250-05905-5
www.picadorusa.com/
howtothinkaboutexercise

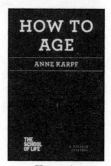

How to Age
Anne Karpf
ISBN 978-1-250-05898-0 / E-ISBN 978-1-250-05899-7
www.picadorusa.com/
howtoage

PICADOR
www.picadorusa.com

Available wherever books and e-books are sold.

Explore All of the "Maintenance Manuals for
the Mind" from the School of Life Library

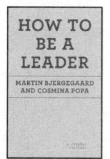

How to Be a Leader
Martin Bjergegaard and Cosmina Popa
ISBN 978-1-250-07873-5
E-ISBN 978-1-250-07874-2

How to Think Like an Entrepeneur
Philip Delves Broughton
ISBN 978-1-250-07871-1
E-ISBN 978-1-250-07872-8

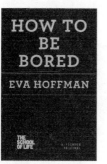

How to Be Bored
Eva Hoffman
ISBN 978-1-250-07867-4
E-ISBN 978-1-250-07868-1

How to Choose a Partner
Susan Quilliam
ISBN 978-1-250-07869-8
E-ISBN 978-1-250-07870-4